HEART SPEAKS TO HEART

HEART SPEAKS TO HEART

Studies in Ecumenical Spirituality

JOHN A NEWTON

DARTON · LONGMAN + TODD

First published in 1994 by
Darton, Longman and Todd Ltd
1 Spencer Court
140–142 Wandsworth High Street
London SW18 4JJ

© 1994 John A Newton

ISBN 0–232–51945–5

Thanks are due for permission to reproduce copyright material:

Bind Us Together, Lord. Copyright © 1977 Thankyou Music, P.O. Box
75, Eastbourne, East Sussex BN23 6NW.

Jesus Is Lord (Creation's Voice Proclaims It) by David Mansell.
Copyright © 1982 Springtide Music/Word Music (UK). Administered
by Copycare Ltd, 8 Marshfoot Lane, Hailsham BN27 2RA.

Lord Jesus Christ. Copyright © 1960 Josef Weinberger Limited.

Spirit of God as Strong as the Wind. Copyright © Scripture Union.

There's a Spirit in the Air by Brian A. Wren (1936–   ) by permission
of Oxford University Press

Phototypeset by Intype, London
Printed and bound in Great Britain
at the University Press, Cambridge

CONTENTS

Acknowledgements   vii

Introduction   1

1 The Heart in Pilgrimage   6

2 The Mersey Miracle   21

3 Edward King and Unity in Christ   30

4 A Tale of Two Bishops   40

5 The Heart Strangely Warmed: a Methodist Response
  to Orthodoxy   53

6 Methodism and Catholicism   68

7 Grasping the Nettle: the Ecumenical Society of the
  Blessed Virgin Mary   85

8 The Common Life in Christ   95

9 One in the Spirit: the Charismatic Movement and
  the Churches   107

  Epilogue   125

  Notes   127

v

ACKNOWLEDGEMENTS

I AM GRATEFUL TO Mrs Mary Jean Pritchard of Darton, Longman and Todd for her advice and encouragement to me in the writing of the following studies. She has been consistently courteous and helpful, and has lifted my drooping spirits on more than one occasion.

Similarly, I am indebted to friends and colleagues who have read parts of the book in draft, and made useful suggestions for its improvement. In particular, I wish to thank Bishop David Sheppard of Liverpool, the Revd Raymond George of Bristol and Mr Brian Frost of London. Needless to say, the responsibility for any remaining faults or errors in the text are mine alone.

My thanks are also due to the members of a number of ecumenical groups who have stimulated my interest in the spirituality of ecumenism. They have done so, not only by asking me from time to time to read them a paper, but also through shared worship, study and friendship. I owe a special debt of gratitude to: The Fellowship of St Alban and St Sergius, the Methodist Sacramental Fellowship, and the Ecumenical Society of the Blessed Virgin Mary. Among the members of these bodies, I have experienced the truth of Archbishop Michael Ramsey's claim that, 'In a depth below doctrinal thought and structure, heart speaks to heart'. This book is in no small part the result of my reflection on that experience.

INTRODUCTION

'I am sure that one of the most hopeful means of realizing Christian unity is for Christians of one tradition to seek to share another tradition's experience of the riches of Christ.'

J. Neville Ward[1]

'We are already one. But we imagine that we are not. It is at the level of doctrinal formulation that we recognize our differences; it is at the level of the religious experience that we come to realize our oneness.'

William H. Shannon[2]

Arthur Michael Ramsey, sometime Archbishop of Canterbury, was an original. His bushy, mobile eyebrows; his quavery voice; his notorious absentmindedness: these all made him a gift to the mimic or parodist. Yet he had an acute mind and great learning. His difficulty, in his early years, lay in making himself understood by all and sundry. As a young clergyman, he served on the staff of Boston parish church, in the Lincolnshire fens. An old parishioner, thirty years later, when Ramsey was Archbishop, recalled his preaching: 'Ah yes, Mr Ramsey; now he was *deep*, very deep. I never understood a word he said, mind you – but he was *deep*.'

Ramsey eventually became a distinguished academic, at both Durham and Cambridge. He could have easily developed, without exerting himself, into a passable imitation of the remote and ineffectual don. To his credit, he

1

did nothing of the kind. Instead, he wrestled with himself until he achieved a lucid simplicity of thought and expression. He became a superb communicator, equally at home in a university mission or a country parish church. For all his greatness of mind, he had something of the child's directness of vision. He would often startle his hearers, and light up their minds, with a vivid fresh insight into the faith he taught. He once extemporized on a theme of St John ('God is light, and in him is no darkness at all'), and produced the unforgettable: 'God is Christ-like, and in him is no un-Christ-likeness at all.'

On another occasion, he was addressing a large ecumenical gathering in Southwell Minister on the theme of Christian unity and the paths that might lead to it. For centuries Christians have discussed, amicably or rancorously, their doctrinal differences. More rarely, they have striven to enlarge their areas of agreement. In the twentieth century they have increasingly worked together in service to society, as in the classic field of Christian Aid. In his sermon, Archbishop Ramsey in no sense disparaged either doctrinal study or social action as roads to unity. He did, however, suggest a third, which he thought was often neglected to our cost. His words, since I first heard them some thirty years ago, have haunted me as a challenge which still needs to be taken up.

The Archbishop was speaking at the First British Faith and Order Conference, in 1964, and his words seemed to me a key which might unlock a door into a large room. He pointed out that,

> In a depth below doctrinal thought and structure, heart speaks to heart. May there not be . . . a similar apartness in the realm of thought and nearness in the depth of religious meaning in the case of some of the cleavages about faith, justification, and the sacraments? I came across recently this remark in the memoirs of the late Father Waggett of Cowley: 'There is no better expression of exactly what we mean by the sacrifice of the Mass than the hymn Rock of Ages.'[3]

Father P. N. Waggett was an Anglo-Catholic, a member of

the Society of St John the Evangelist, colloquially known as the Cowley Fathers. The author of the hymn 'Rock of Ages' was also an Anglican clergyman, but of a very different stamp from Philip Waggett. Augustus Montague Toplady (1740–1778) was an ultra-Protestant, whose militant Calvinism led him into violent controversy with fellow-Anglicans like John Wesley; and to bracket him with the Cowley Fathers seems at first sight like yoking together Ian Paisley and the Pope. Certainly Waggett's remark raises many questions about 'faith, justification, and the sacraments'.

Yet Waggett was not being provocative. He was sincere in detecting a resonance between the hymn 'Rock of Ages' and the sacrifice of the Mass. The two come from widely separated ecclesiastical traditions. There seems to be a great gulf fixed between them. Waggett's words, however, are not simply a pathetic attempt to throw a slender rope across an unbridgeable chasm. Toplady's hymn majors on justification by faith. The believer is nothing, has nothing, in himself. He simply casts himself on the mercy of Christ crucified.

> Rock of Ages, cleft for me,
> Let me hide myself in thee;
> Let the water and the blood,
> From thy riven side which flowed,
> Be of sin the double cure,
> Cleanse me from its guilt and power.

With Toplady's 'Nothing in my hand I bring,/Simply to thy cross I cling', we may compare the language of the Mass. The words are very different, but is what Ramsey calls 'the depth of religious meaning' so alien to what Toplady intends? In the Mass, as the worshipper looks to the Crucified, s/he confesses, 'Lord, I am not worthy to receive you; but only say the word, and I shall be healed.' Anglo-Catholic and Calvinist meet at the cross. Both depend utterly on the divine mercy. 'Rock of Ages' and the sacrifice of the Mass both proclaim the totally undeserved mercy of God.

In such ways, 'heart speaks to heart.' But what of the hard doctrinal issues that must be faced in any search for Christian unity which has integrity? If we follow this path of spirituality, are we not simply trying to by-pass the obstacles? If we open our hearts, are we not in danger of closing our minds? These are proper questions, which warn of real pitfalls. To answer them, we need to go back to Archbishop Ramsey's sermon. When he declared, 'Heart speaks to heart', he was citing John Henry Newman, who chose these words as his motto when he was made cardinal. Clearly in doing so he meant no disparagement of the intellect. If ever a Christian sought to love God with his whole mind, it was Newman. Yet he saw that people are more than their minds. It is the whole man or woman who believes or disbelieves, not just their intellect. Newman never forgot the biblical meaning of 'heart' as the central core of the personality. The 'heart' is not a synonym for the emotions. It comprehends feeling, intellect, imagination and will. So, when the teacher of Proverbs says to the young man, 'My son, give me your *heart*' (Proverbs 23:26), he is calling for a total response of the personality.

That being so, 'heart speaks to heart' is not a glib formula for Christian unity. It is not a primrose path to unity without tears. On the contrary, it requires the grace of the Holy Spirit, the great Interpreter, who can break through the barriers of custom and stereotype, and enable mutual understanding. Indeed, we may need a conversion of heart and mind if we are to encounter one another at the deepest levels of the life of devotion. What Charles Wesley says of our encounter with God, we may apply to our meeting with Christians of a tradition far removed from our own:

> Lord, my time is in thy hand,
>   My soul to thee convert;
> Thou canst make me understand,
>   Though I am slow of heart . . .[4]

If we are to understand our fellow Christians at more than the most superficial level, we shall need the gifts of empathy, discernment, imagination, and the ability to 'translate' what we see and hear with truthfulness and sensitivity.

4

In the chapters that follow, I shall try to detect spiritual resonances of the kind that Father Waggett suggests. I shall extrapolate both from the history of the Church and from contemporary Christian experience. I believe there is no lack of material from either source. Indeed, I think it possible that future investigation may show a rich seam to be mined in the field of ecumenical spirituality. It may well prove as productive as the work of the Alister Hardy Research Centre, which investigates the prevalence of distinctively religious experience. The Alister Hardy team was surprised at the widespread response to its enquiries. I suspect that, when we look carefully for occasions when 'heart speaks to heart', we may find that here, too, there is God's plenty.

1

THE HEART IN PILGRIMAGE

THE LINCOLNSHIRE TOWN where I grew up is islanded on one side by the Wash, and on the other by the Fens, which stretch away like a lesser sea to an illimitable distance. 'Flat land makes flat people,' our Yorkshire Latin master used to lay down as a self-evident principle; and though we scorned his dogmatism, we were hardly in a position to challenge it. Yet if the topography of Boston was comparatively featureless – apart from the marvellous skyscapes – the religious terrain most certainly was not. Though a country town of modest size – 28,000 people – Boston was certainly not monochrome in religion. There was a sprinkling of Jewish families, though far too few to warrant a synagogue. There was a small Roman Catholic church, St Mary's, at the far end of the town, with Father Bernard Grimley as its devoted parish priest. He became nationally known through his radio talks, and I still recall how movingly he spoke of his parents' conversion to Catholicism through an Italian Mission to England. The 'Italian Mission', of course, was how some Protestants disparagingly referred to the Roman Catholic Church itself, at least as found in these islands. Father Grimley's testimony gave me a new respect for that Church and its faithful. One branch of our own family consisted of Irish Catholics, who were members of his congregation. Yet I never once saw inside his church, nor had the remotest idea of the worship that took place within it.

The Anglican parish churches in the town could cope with most forms of churchmanship to be found under the broad umbrella of the Church of England. St Thomas' was Anglo-Catholic. St Nicholas' was also High Church, and perched perilously close to the estuary, where the River Witham flows down to the sea. It stood perennially at risk from any repetition of 'The High Tide on the Coast of Lincolnshire', so vividly described by the Boston poet, Jean Ingelow.

Holy Trinity was Evangelical. But the pride of the whole town was the supremely magnificent parish church of St Botolph ('Boston Stump', in the splendid understatement of the natives). Its great tower is visible for twenty miles across the surrounding fen country, or from the cliffs of Hunstanton on the other side of the Wash. The Stump, like its daughter churches of St James and St Christopher, was High rather than Low, as befitted a church of cathedral proportions, but not stridently so. It was basically central Anglican in worship and churchmanship, and was served by some outstandingly able clergy.

Then there were the Methodist chapels, thickly strewn throughout the town and its environs. They were varied in both architecture and tradition – Wesleyan, Primitive and United Methodist. There were six of them in the town itself, and a score or more in the surrounding countryside. Lincoln was John Wesley's own county, and this was Methodist heartland. There were some lively and devoted societies (congregations), as there still are; but resources tended to be spread thinly over a very wide area, which did not make it easy either to consolidate or advance.

Other Free Churches in the town included: the Salvation Army citadel; a Congregational church, served by a devoted and scholarly minister, the Reverend R. E. Thomas. He had been trained at Mansfield College, Oxford, was steeped in prayer, and never shirked the humblest pastoral chores. A Baptist church in the High Street prided itself on a 300-year existence since the Commonwealth. There were also small Elim (Pentecostal) and Christadelphian congregations tucked away in corners of the town.

These differing traditions of Christianity, though living cheek by jowl in a small and friendly community, very rarely interacted with each other. For the most part, it was live and let live; you have your church, I have mine; and everyone to his or her choice. The Free Churches would occasionally come together on Maundy Thursday or Good Friday. On a major civic or national occasion – a mayor-making, the end of the War – there would be a great service for the whole town in St Botolph's. As a boy in the First Boston Sea Scouts, I attended numerous such services, on church parade, bands playing and flags flying, as we marched across the wide expanse of the marketplace to the parish church.

Undoubtedly, however, for me the Christian Church meant, primarily, Zion Methodist Church, Brothertoft Road, Boston West, just half a mile from home. It was there I attended Sunday school (morning and afternoon), joined the youth club, was received into church membership, learned to speak in public and help conduct worship, trained as a lay preacher. It was there I received from older members of the church kindness and encouragement, in good gospel measure – full, pressed down and running over. I had never had instilled into me, that I can recall,the slightest dislike of Christians of other communions. They simply did not impinge. We were Methodists; they were otherwise – good folk, no doubt, but their ways were different. As Wesley's 'people called Methodists', we treasured our heritage of faith and worship, and gloried especially in our hymns. We cherished a preaching tradition, both lay and ministerial, which, if it could at times sink into bathos, more commonly challenged and fortified the hearers. Our sacramental practice was simple and devout, with normally a monthly service of Holy Communion. On New Year's Eve, we faithfully observed the Watchnight Service, Wesley's repristination of the early Christian Vigil. On the first Sunday of the New Year, we held a solemn Covenant Service, for our rededication to God's service in Christ's way. Its prayer of consecration searched us to the depths, as each worshipper, after rigorous self-examination, made the profession:

> I am no longer my own, but Thine. Put me to what Thou wilt, rank me with whom Thou wilt. Put me to doing, put me to suffering; let me have all things, let

8

me have nothing. I freely and heartily yield all things to Thy pleasure and disposal . . .

The Church of South India, formed in 1947 by Anglicans, Methodists, Presbyterians, and Congregationalists, took over the Covenant Service as part of its liturgy. It was duly incorporated in the Church's Book of Common Worship of 1963.[1] Yet it would be a fairly safe bet that few of the Lincolnshire Methodists who nurtured my own faith, would have dreamed of such a borrowing. It is a moot point which would have been less likely – Methodists offering, or other Christians accepting, a form of service which seemed so peculiarly our own.

It was not that we were in any sense at daggers drawn with other Christians. They went their way, and we ours, to the City of God at the other end of the road. There were many pathways, but they did not usually intersect. We would commonly acknowledge that we were all going to the same place; but we were not pilgrims together.

All this was changed when at nineteen I went away to college. University College, Hull, was only sixty miles from Boston, via Grimsby and the New Holland ferry across the Humber. Geographically speaking, I was still only marginally outside the county boundary. (Local government reorganization had not yet filched South Humberside from Lincolnshire.) Yet in religious, as well as in academic terms, the city of Kingston-upon-Hull was a whole world away from the market town of Boston.

I was due to read for a history degree, and had made a start on preliminary reading. Before I left home for my first term at college, I cycled over to Kirton – one of the villages in the Boston Methodist Circuit – to return a clutch of history books lent me by the scholarly minister there, Raymond Blackburn. Raymond was a remarkably gifted person. He was still young, not long back then from the war – this was in 1949 – where he had served as a chaplain with the Eighth Army. He was musical, with a fine tenor voice, and I can hear him now singing songs like 'Linden Lea' and 'Silent Worship', which he did with a purity of tone that spurned all sentimentality. He was well read, and preached like an angel. At the same time, he was extraordinarily practical. He was a do-it-yourself man before the term became current, and regularly serviced his own car and carried out repairs. He reminds me of the great Irish Methodist scholar, Dr Adam Clarke, who believed that 'Methodist preachers ... should ... be capable of assisting themselves in every way because of the peculiar situations in which they are placed.' Clarke claimed, with some pride: 'I can build a haystack or a chimney-piece; mend my own shoes; put sleeves into my own coat, repair a frying pan, put bars to a gridiron and turn a lathe'.[2] Ray Blackburn was of the same breed. He spent all his ministry in country circuits, knew flowers and trees, and was a good amateur ornithologist.

When I took him back his books, he gave me an encouraging word and wished me well as I embarked on three years' study for the London history degree. His parting words, spoken over forty years ago now, still ring true: 'I envy you, you know, John. I would give anything to have a chance to study for three years, especially history. And yet I think you'll find, at the end of the course, that you've only pushed open the gate to a very large field.'

That made sound academic sense; but on reflection it was also true of my religious experience. Here too a very large field opened out. I met species of Christians unknown to me before. Anglo-Catholics, Quakers, Welsh Independents, Strict and Particular Baptists, Roman Catholics, and rabid Fundamentalists: all these and more suddenly swam into my ken. In those days, University College Hull did not have a plethora of denominational student societies. The Roman Catholics had their own grouping, but for the rest, the Christian societies comprised simply the Student Christian Movement (mildly liberal) and the Christian Union (conservative). At first, I naively assumed it was possible to be a member of both; but the CU representative soon disabused me of that idea, and so I opted for the SCM.

The branch membership consisted mainly of Anglicans (High and Low) Presbyterians, Congregationalists, Methodists and Quakers. The Baptists seemed usually to gravitate to the Christian Union. We held midday prayers for staff and students in The Sanctuary, a plain but decent hut on the main campus. Here I encountered forms of devotion that were entirely new to me. High Anglicans would devoutly cross themselves, and pray 'by the book'. Quakers would initiate us into a pattern of quietness, which involved 'centring down' into a deep silence in the presence of God.

Both forms of worship were a far cry from the services I had been reared in through my native Methodism. We formed preaching bands and led services in local churches, which took a great deal of preparation. We would hammer out a pattern of worship that incorporated elements of our diverse traditions, and serve up the liturgical goulash as reverently as we could. Whatever the congregations gained, we ourselves certainly profited by the exercise. Prayers like the General Thanksgiving from the Book of Common Prayer took on new significance after we had heard an Anglican student expound the depth of meaning it had for her own spiritual life.

This blitz of new religious impressions was bewildering at first. Yet one of the great strengths of SCM was that, though thoroughly ecumenical, it never encouraged students to become 'un-denominational' in their religious practice. We were consistently urged never to sit light to our own tradition of faith and life. On the contrary, we were left in no doubt that our prime duty, as would-be ecumenists, was to be faithful, informed, committed members of our own church. So I must first be a good Methodist. That was both reassuring and disturbing. It was reassuring because it affirmed my previous Christian formation. It was disturbing because, though not very theologically literate, I was often expected to expound the Methodist Church's doctrinal position. At one SCM Bible School, the Reverend James McEwen, a learned Church of Scotland theologian, had a bone to pick with John Wesley over his doctrine of Christian Perfection, which Wesley had made central to Methodist teaching. Before excoriating Wesley, he challenged the Methodists present to identify themselves. He then shamed us by his ready assumption that we would have not the slightest difficulty in expounding and defending Wesley's view.

It was a salutory lesson for me to realize that if I were really committed to Christian unity, I must know where I stood in my own tradition. How else could I make any contribution to the 'Coming Great Church'? Moreover, I must be rooted not simply in doctrine, but in the worship, prayer and devotion which characterized my Church. I felt on somewhat surer ground here. At least I could expound something of the meaning of Holy Communion in Methodism, the Wesley hymns, the Covenant and Watchnight services. These had been bred in me, and had become part of my living experience of the faith.

It was not enough, however, in SCM terms, to know your own churchmanship, and be firmly grounded in your faith. You were urged to be genuinely open to receive from others, who had very different ways of being Christian to share. At first blush, you might be repelled by aspects of Christian practice quite alien to your own experience, just as others might be by yours. No matter; you were pledged to go on listening and learning, trying to see Christ through the eyes of other Christians.

SCM taught me other lessons. It made crystal clear the need for intellectual integrity in holding the Christian faith. We were to love God with all our mind. Christ was the Lord of thought. That meant that our degree work was a central part of our offering to him. So there could be no question of excusing a poor degree by pleading that the Lord had called you to concentrate on more 'Christian work'. For a Christian student, the study of history, economics, or biology, *was* the Lord's work, and you were to do it with all your ability. By the same token, the intellectual rigour of the lecture-room and seminar must be brought to Bible study or to the making of a sermon in the preaching band. The universe of thought was one, and Christ was to be honoured in the whole of it. So, though at this time I was no theological student, I found myself, in SCM groups, studying some of the key ethical and theological texts of the 1950s. Sir Walter Moberly's *Crisis in the University*; Oscar Cullmann's *Christ and*

12

Time, Alan Richardson's *Theological Wordbook of the Bible*: all these made their contribution.

SCM also put me in its debt by opening up the whole enormous realm of the arts in relation to Christianity. That was not an area, in my youth at least, in which Methodists majored. I had almost everything to learn. In my first year at Hull, Professor John Tinsley, head of the Department of Theology and a Senior Friend of SCM, gave a superb series of slide-illustrated lectures on 'Christianity and the Arts'. He ransacked the riches of Christendom in painting, sculpture and architecture. To one student at least, the effect was revelatory. Boston Grammar School gave its pupils a good all-round literary and scientific education. Yet, with all its virtues, it laid little emphasis on aesthetics. SCM helped supply that serious deficiency. At the Bible School at Courteenhall, Northants, where James McEwen had exposed my ignorance of the finer points of Wesleyan theology, our studies were by no means solely biblical. From Courteenhall House, we bussed into Northampton, to the Anglican parish church of St Matthew, whose incumbent Walter Hussey (later Dean of Chichester) was an ardent patron of the arts. We saw in his church Graham Sutherland's tortured painting of the Crucifixion, and gazed on the still, unravished bride of quietness that is Henry Moore's Madonna and Child. It was a new experience to see major works of art sited, not as museum pieces, but in the house of God, speaking of his glory, in the context of his people's worship.

After graduating at Hull, I was fortunate in having my state scholarship renewed to undertake research with Professor Geoffrey Dickens, a distinguished Reformation scholar, who had recently returned to his native Hull from Keble College, Oxford. My chosen field was Roman Catholic recusancy and Puritan nonconformity in the early seventeenth-century diocese of York. Surprisingly, there were contacts between these two opposite ends of the ecclesiastical spectrum, and not only in polemical debate. Indeed, one Yorkshire Puritan minister, Edmund Bunney, actually adapted a Jesuit catechism for use with his own people, copyright then being no impediment. I was equally interested in both recusants

13

and nonconformists, many of whom I came to know by name. The University of London, however, thought otherwise, and served me with a writ of 'Choose this day whom you will serve.' It was not an easy choice, but in the end I opted for the Puritans. I was nearer to them by tradition, since Wesley drew extensively on the Puritan divines, and I had then little living contact with Catholicism. Moreover, Professor Dickens had already done a good deal of pioneering work on the Elizabethan Puritans of Yorkshire, and there was a rich seam waiting to be worked for the seventeenth century.

Yet I dropped my Catholic recusants with genuine regret. Before I abandoned them at the dictates of the university, I had ventured in search of material into the library of Endsleigh Teacher Training College. The college was staffed by a teaching order of nuns, and I found myself for the first time inside a Roman Catholic institution. The sisters were in every way helpful, and yet as a Protestant I felt like a fish out of water. I was conscious that, but for the purposes of academic research, I should never have thought of entering the place. So much about the institution was entirely strange: the frequent crucifixes, the statues, the sisters themselves in their traditional habits. It was as though I had entered a different world. I felt a distinct *frisson* each time I went into the college; a sense that I was being greatly daring, possibly foolhardy, and in some obscure way jeopardizing the purity of my Protestant faith. These reactions, as I now realize, were bred of fear out of ignorance, and largely instinctive. They seem almost laughable now, but they were real enough at the time. I mention them simply to underline how high were the barriers between separated Christians in the early 1950s, before – thanks to Pope John XXIII – the walls came tumbling down.

If my research into recusancy brought me closer to Catholics, my Puritan studies indirectly introduced me to the thought and practice of the Quakers. Already, through the work of SCM, I had met Roger Wilson, head of the Department of Social Studies in the university, and an outstanding Quaker. My horizons widened as a research student, as I travelled daily from Hull to York, to work on the rich collection of ecclesiastical records housed in the recently-founded Borthwick Institute of Historical Research on Pease-holme Green.

York was not only the centre of the Northern Province of the Church of England; it was also a fertile seedbed of the Religious Society of Friends. The Quaker dynasties of Terrys and Rowntrees had set their distinctive mark of philanthropy on the life of the city, which boasted two fine schools established by the Friends – The Mount and Bootham. Through the kindness of a college friend doing teaching practice at Bootham School, I was able to eat my packed lunch there most days while I was working in York. I learned of the Quaker simplicity and integrity, which eschewed rank and status, and encouraged the young student teacher to address the headmaster simply as 'Martin Green'. From this contact with one Quaker institution, I was soon led to another. My research took me to London to the British Museum Reading Room, to comb through the writings of the seventeenth-century Yorkshire Puritans, who were now my prime quarry. I stayed at the Friends' International Centre, then housed in Tavistock Square. Here I was received with the same unpretentious kindness that I had known from the Catholic nuns in Hull. I was also invited to share, for fifteen minutes each morning, in worship 'after the manner of Friends'.

In that worship, the silence was palpable. A small group of us simply sat around a table, on which were placed a Bible and a book of readings. Occasionally, someone would pray aloud, read a passage from Scripture, or quote from the Quaker writings. Mostly, we were entirely quiet; but there was a depth and richness to the silence that I had hardly known before. Later, at theological college in Cambridge, I came to know the hymn of Charles Wesley which speaks of that same quality of silence. Wesley takes the account of Elijah's experience on Mount Horeb of the 'still small voice', after the cannonade of the storm. Its words often reminded me of that silent worship of the Friends:

15

> Open, Lord, my inward ear,
>   And bid my heart rejoice;
> Bid my quiet spirit hear
>   Thy comfortable voice;
> Never in the whirlwind found,
>   Or where earthquakes rock the place,
> Still and silent is the sound,
>   The whisper of thy grace.[3]

The silent Orders of the Catholic Church – Trappists and Carthusians – have made of this approach to God a whole way of life. Yet they have never claimed a monopoly of it. The Friends brought home to me the truth that it is open to any Christian to know something of the power of silence in the life of grace.

The ten years after I left Hull in 1953 saw no lessening of my ecumenical commitment, but my work, in a series of Methodist institutions, helped to deepen my grasp of my own tradition. I became more self-consciously – though not, I trust, more narrowly – Methodist. I tried to heed Wesley's call to his followers to demonstrate what he calls 'Catholic spirit' towards other Christians, and to show themselves 'the friends of all, the enemies of none'. This double commitment to Methodism and ecumenism was symbolized for me by joining the Methodist Sacramental Fellowship. The twin aims of this body are to pray and work for renewal in Methodism, and for the visible reunion of Christ's Church. In the words of the Fellowship prayer:

> Almighty God, who raised up your servants John and Charles Wesley to proclaim anew the gift of redemption and the life of holiness, be with us their children and revive your work among us; that inspired by the same faith and upheld by the same grace in Word and Sacrament, we and all your people may be made one in the unity of Christ's Church on earth, even as in heaven we are made one in him; who is alive and reigns with you and the Holy Spirit, one God, now and for ever. Amen.

My encounters with Catholics in Hull, and Quakers in

16

York, were followed by an experience of the Reformed tradition when I moved, in 1953, to London. While working in the university's Institute of Historical Research, I lodged at New College in Hampstead. New College – now shared between Westfield College and the Open University – was then a Congregational theological college, and a constituent member of the university's Divinity School. The newly-appointed principal was the Reverend John Huxtable, fresh from an outstanding ministry at Palmer's Green and wholly committed to the ecumenical vision. He, his colleagues and students, all treated me as one of themselves, though I was not an ordinand, and I owe them an inestimable debt. Dr Geoffrey Nuttall, the college's Tutor in Church History, was a Puritan scholar of international stature, and freely allowed me to draw on his formidable store of learning. I shared so fully in the life of the college that, when I eventually offered as a candidate for the Methodist ministry, my record led one member of the final selection committee to ask pointedly: 'I was interested to hear you speak of the closeness of fellowship at New College. Are you sure your call is to the Methodist ministry and not to the Congregational?' I was sure, but the debt to Congregationalism was an enduring one. It has left me with a scattering of friends across the country who are now ministers of the United Reformed Church.

My Methodist life, and indeed my call to the ministry, was more directly nurtured at Hinde Street Methodist Church, where the late Dr Arthur Shaw was chaplain to Methodist students in the university. Here I found classic Methodism in the Wesleyan tradition. The Order of Morning Prayer was in regular use. There was both a strong sacramental tradition and scholarly, biblical preaching. Class meetings and house groups flourished; and there was a strong ministry of outreach and caring to the local hospitals, the colleges of the university, and the neighbouring West End. Arthur Shaw himself was pure gold: an ex-RAF chaplain, young, eager, a born leader – he had been Chairman of his college at Richmond – and a great enabler and encourager. His influence for good on hundreds of young lives was quite incalculable. It was through his ministerial example – I have never known

17

a finer one – and a Trinity Sunday sermon he preached on 'Called to be an apostle . . .' – that I was led to offer for the Christian ministry.

Then followed a six-year spell in various Methodist institutions. I did an emergency stint for a year as acting chaplain at Kent College, Canterbury. That proved a useful preparation for two years' theological training at Wesley House, Cambridge. I was next appointed as an assistant tutor at Richmond College, Surrey, to teach Greek, New Testament and Plato's *Republic*, an agreeable mix. The college was perched on the top of Richmond Hill, a stone's throw from the Terrace with its classic view of the Thames. Among the senior staff were Dr Harold Roberts, the principal, and Dr Marcus Ward, recently back from distinguished service in the Church of South India. Both men were involved in the negotiations for Anglican-Methodist unity, and were acutely disappointed when the scheme failed to carry in 1972.

Richmond deepened my understanding of Methodism, and my appreciation of what was best in its life. The college maintained a high standard of worship and preaching, and was noted both for scholarship and for an outstanding tradition of missionary service. The young Dietrich Bonhoeffer, then minister to a German congregation in South London, visited the college in 1938. The author of *The Cost of Discipleship* was deeply moved by the great boards in the college entrance hall, which recorded the early deaths of so many of the young men who had gone to serve in West Africa in the 1840s.

That missionary tradition was visibly embodied on the staff by Clive Thexton, who had served in Ceylon, and by Marcus Ward, who had given nearly a quarter of a century to the Christian Church in South India. It was Marcus Ward, Methodist minister and presbyter of the Church of South India, who gave my ecumenism a sharper focus. He was an outstanding ecumenical statesman. He had been one of the architects of the recently united Church of South India, and had he stayed in India would almost certainly have been made one of her bishops. He brought with him all his love and experience of India. A constant stream of visitors from

18

the sub-continent, former colleagues and students, beat a way to the door of his manse, and enriched the life of the college community. He introduced a number of us to the novels of John Masters, set in British India, and would say, 'When I read those books, I can see, taste and smell India.' That no doubt was a tribute to Masters' artistry; but it also speaks eloquently of Marcus's passionate love of the land.

Marcus Ward also shared with us his living experience of a united Church. He made us realize that the ecumenical quest was no pipe dream. It had substance and it had hope. Utterly loyal son of John Wesley that he was, he would confess from time to time, 'I find it hard to revert to denominationalism.' In the deepest sense, in his life of prayer, his spirituality, his formation as a Christian man, he never did. He was perhaps the most complete ecumenist I have ever known. He was a standing witness to the truth that genuine coming together in Christ, far from diminishing, enormously enriches, the common life of Christians.

Students would ask him to preside at a celebration of the Church of South India Eucharist, usually timed for early morning, and always well attended. It was not the exchange of his black Methodist robes for the white cassock of CSI that chiefly impressed – though that was memorable, in imparting a note of light and joy sometimes lacking in Protestant worship. It was much more the liturgy itself, with its interweaving of early Christian prayers, its inclusion of the Peace, and its refusal to separate Word and Sacrament. However limited the time, Marcus would always give a brief but pungent homily on one of the lections, and link it to the action of the sacrament. He was a lifelong member of the Methodist Sacramental Fellowship, which prayed characteristically that God would renew his people by 'the same grace in Word and Sacrament'. The CSI liturgy in his hands became a living embodiment of that ideal. As an experience of the Christian Eucharist – its universality, its joy, its renewing power – it was deeply satisfying, unforgettable. I could understand why the celebrant had found it hard to 'revert

19

to denominationalism'. Who would not have done, after that?

Marcus Ward's influence confirmed me in my convictions as a Methodist minister. It also made me more sure than ever that I could not be content to be simply a Methodist. I must be true to the ecumenical vision and seek the unity of Christ's Church.

2

THE MERSEY MIRACLE

BETWEEN LEAVING RICHMOND in 1961, and going north to Liverpool in 1986, there intervened a quarter of a century of pastoral and teaching experience. My work took me in turn to Louth, in rural Lincolnshire; to Stockton, on industrial Tees-side; to Bristol, for twelve years on the staff of Wesley College in its work of training ministers; to Kenya and the ecumenical theological college of St Paul's, Limuru; and finally to the capital, for eight years' work in the West London Mission. Yet Liverpool, as the Americans say, was really something else.

When asked to go as Chairman of the Liverpool District of the Methodist Church, I consented, though not without fear and trembling. My previous, limited experience of the city had certainly been favourable. I was ordained in Liverpool, when the Methodist Conference met there in 1960, and had been impressed by the noble waterfront, with its striking cluster of public buildings. I still cherished the memory of the ecumenical service held in the as yet only half-built Anglican Cathedral. In 1975, when Conference again met in Liverpool, there was another crowded and jubilant ecumenical celebration in the Roman Catholic Metropolitan Cathedral, at the other end of Hope Street.

On both occasions we encountered the wit and exuberance, the warmth and friendliness of the Merseyside people. Kenneth Waights, a distinguished minister who had served in Liverpool during the Second World War, recalled the experience in an article written for the Conference Handbook in 1975. Not even the German bombing could quench the Liverpool humour of the war years. He recalled the old

21

couple who were making their way down the steps of a tenement block, after the air-raid sirens had just wailed out their warning. They were half-way down to the basement shelter, when the old man stopped abruptly: 'Eh, Mam, I shall have to go back – I've left me teeth up in the flat.' 'Don't be so daft,' the old lady rejoined, 'it's bombs they're dropping, not sandwiches!'

Yet, though my previous impressions of Liverpool had been uniformly good, they were at least ten years old. Since my last stay in the city, in 1975, there had been great fallings-off. Liverpool had been smitten by economic decline, severe urban decay, the serious riots of 1981, and fierce political in-fighting. On the last score, a Militant-dominated City Council had made Liverpool a byword for extremism and confrontation. I was soon to learn that there was another side to the political imbroglio, and that central government policies had in a measure pushed Liverpool into a corner, making it virtually certain that it would take off its coat and fight. Nevertheless, viewed from London, where I was working, and given the jaundiced image of the city portrayed by the media, to move there with a family was not an altogether inviting prospect.

The reaction of friends and colleagues to the prospective move from south-east to north-west, London to Liverpool, was interesting and varied. One colleague frankly commiserated with me: 'Sorry to hear about your bed of nails.' Others simply raised their eyebrows to a height that conveyed more than many words. Yet for all the surface misgivings which these reactions provoked, I was not discouraged. I knew the shadow side of the city's life was real and disturbing; but I also knew there was a new world which had been called into being to redress the balance of the old. Another colleague, born and bred in Liverpool, encouraged me by his account of a great change for the better that had come over the city in his lifetime. 'If you'd told me', he volunteered, 'thirty-five years ago, when I was a lad growing up in Liverpool, that I would ever live to see the day when Catholics and Protestants would work in close partnership, I would have thought you'd taken leave of your senses.' If one aspect of miracle is that it comes out of the blue, against all expectations, and takes your breath away, then, yes, we can properly speak about a miracle on the river Mersey.

A few months before I was due to leave London for Liverpool, I heard an account of the miracle from one who had been at the centre of it: Bishop David Sheppard. He was speaking at a lunch-hour meeting in the church of St James, Piccadilly. A questioner put it to him that Liverpool was a terrible place to live in. 'Not at all,' said Bishop David. 'My wife wouldn't live anywhere else; she wants to die in Liverpool.' He went on to give an account of the energy and vitality of the people of the city, and of the renewal of its community and religious life. Time was when Protestants and Catholics existed virtually in separate armed camps. The city had most of the makings of a Belfast-style confrontation. It had a long history of religious bigotry; a large population of Irish descent; housing segregation on sectarian lines; and a Protestant political party which dominated its civic life. All that provides the context for a piece of folklore which throws a lurid light on the religious temper of Liverpool only a generation or two ago. It concerns the strange anomaly of a mixed marriage which apparently worked. A devout Catholic woman had been married for many years to an equally fervent Protestant husband. In their terraced house, above the living-room fireplace, two pictures hung: one of the Pope, another of King William III, the archetypal Protestant hero. Visitors were amazed to see this conjunction of portraits, and would ask, 'How do you live together? Don't you have rows?' 'Yes,' said the old lady, 'sometimes we do.' 'What happens then?' 'Well, when we have a real row, my old man takes down the picture of the Pope and goes and pawns him.' 'What do you do then?' 'While he's out of the house, I takes down the picture of King Billy, and I goes and pawns him; and with what I gets for King Billy, I redeems the Pope!' It may be folklore, but in essence it rings true.

It would be foolish, of course, to pretend that Liverpool has been purged of all trace of bigotry. The miracle does not extend that far. Yet you would have to be purblind not to recognize that, religiously speaking, there has been a sea-change on the Mersey. A great tide of charity, understanding and co-operation has swept through the life of the Christian churches – Roman Catholic, Anglican, and Nonconformist. An indispensable lead has been given by Archbishop Derek Worlock and Bishop David Sheppard, who by the grace of God have broken down generations of mistrust. The new spirit is embodied also in the wider Church Leaders' Group, and in the various agencies of the Merseyside and Region Churches' Ecumenical Assembly. Nor has the movement stopped there. If you want to make it real, make it local. That is the proverbial wisdom, and it is one that has caught on with Liverpool Christians. The new spirit of unity has put down deep roots at the level of parish and congregation. The movement from the top down has met an eager and joyful response from the bottom up. Yet 'up' and 'down' are perhaps misleading terms here. It would be truer to say that the Spirit has been working like yeast, across and within the Christian churches, fermenting with new life.

Christianity is about miracle – the miracle of God's grace and love, transforming situations which seem so hopelessly embittered as to be beyond redemption. It is also about resurrection, renewal, life from the dead, the rekindling of hope. What has happened on Merseyside has the marks of resurrection and new life written all over it. Certainly many outside the city, as well as within it, have seen Liverpool as a portent. It has become a much-needed sign of hope within the wider movement for Christian unity which at times has seemed to be slowing down, or even grinding to a halt.

When on 8th September, 1990, the Council of Churches for Britain and Ireland was inaugurated, Liverpool seemed the natural choice for the venue. Those who chose it might have argued that it was suitable on simple geographical grounds. After all, here was a new international body for the churches of England, Scotland, Wales and Ireland. Liverpool enjoys a reasonably central position within the whole British Isles. Why look further? Yet it was not simply a geographical choice. Those who selected the city recognized that Liverpool had been enabled to break new ground ecumenically.

24

The ground had certainly been stonily resistant in the past. All the more remarkable, then, that this stubborn backwater of sectarianism had been transfigured into a sign of Christian unity, a promise of better things to come. So the choice of the city to inaugurate a forward-looking ecumenical council made the clearest sense.

One of the symbols of the new thing which under God has been happening among Christians in Liverpool is the great Pentecost celebration, held every other year on Whitsunday afternoon. As a newcomer, my first experience of it fell in 1987 when, as Free Church Moderator for Merseyside, I took my place with the Bishops at the head of the procession. Church people in their thousands first packed the Anglican Cathedral for worship and celebration. Then we processed along Hope Street to the Catholic Cathedral Church of Christ the King at the other end of this aptly named thoroughfare. We set off with banners waving, Salvation Army band playing fortissimo, and the people singing heartily, 'Onward, Christian soldiers' and 'Bind us together, Lord, bind us together with love'.

But it was not to be all plain sailing. As we left the Anglican Cathedral, Archbishop Derek said to me, 'Let's see, this is your first time, isn't it? We should have warned you, there'll be a reception committee waiting for us round the corner.' There was. As we moved joyfully from the Cathedral into Hope Street, we were met by a small knot of demonstrators. They were no more than two dozen, including a few children, dragged along at their parents' chariot wheels. Like most demonstrators, their noise was out of all proportion to their numbers. They bawled and jeered, and generally execrated us and all our works. We were guilty, apparently, of betraying the Bible, the gospel, and the Christian religion. They spat at the three of us leading the procession, and as we sang on regardless, they assured us, with relish, 'You'll not be singing in hell!' If it had not been so tragic, it would have been ludicrous. They were undoubtedly sincere, but yet prepared to play such fantastic tricks before high heaven as make the angels weep.

The ecumenical movement is not immune from criticism;

nor should it claim to be. On the contrary, it should welcome reasoned argument and informed debate; but vilification and rank abuse are another thing altogether. However, such a throw-back to an age when malice and all uncharitableness were common form can serve to remind us how far we have come, and how much we have to be thankful for. Some of the demonstrators, as already noted, had brought their children with them. Nevertheless, they laid no credible claim to the future, with their bitter insistence on 'old, unhappy far-off things, and battles long ago'. They certainly did not represent the great mass of Christian people on Merseyside, who bore their abuse with good humour, as they pressed on along the street called Hope, as pilgrims together.

Having briefly sketched the background to our ecumenical work in Liverpool, I turn now to its outworking in practice. I have learned from Archbishop Derek and Bishop David to think of ecumenical activity as a threefold cord. Its strands are spiritual, doctrinal and social. They may be separated in thought, but they need to be intertwined in practice. In this study I have chosen to concentrate on spiritual ecumenism. In doing so, I have emphatically no intention of trying to divorce this aspect of work for unity from the other two. A threefold cord cannot be so easily broken.

Sixty years ago, it was fashionable for Christians who sought unity to play off doctrine (Faith and Order) against Christian service (Life and Work). The simplistic slogan was coined, 'Doctrine divides, service unites.' Superficially that may be true, but it cannot stand up to serious scrutiny. Christians soon found that when they co-operated on practical forms of service, doctrinal and moral issues had a way of springing up unexpectedly and setting them at odds. They still do, when for example Christians try to tackle jointly such issues as abortion, Aids, or bio-ethics. The inter-church body COMPASS (Counselling on Merseyside and Pastoral Support Service) has done sterling work in training counsellors and helping individuals with advice and support. Yet it is not just a practical piece of social service which happens to be run by the churches. It raises theological questions, because it springs from a Christian view of the human person

– and Christians may not always see eye to eye on that – in its detailed implications for counselling. Is COMPASS, for example, just providing an anodyne, helping people to become 'adjusted' to a quality of life which is sub-Christian, or to a state of society which in some ways is radically unjust? Alternatively, along with its valuable work of healing and support, should COMPASS also be fostering a divine discontent with things as they are? These are theological as well as practical questions, and they suggest that it is neither easy nor wise for Christians to try to separate doctrinal from practical ecumenism.

Again, Aids raises issues which are both acutely practical, and profoundly theological. On the one hand, there is an enormous need for practical care and compassion. Christians working with Aids sufferers on Merseyside have identified an acute need for residential care for some who are terminally ill. Those who have no family, or whose family may have rejected them, are especially vulnerable to loneliness and despair. Some of the religious houses and communities on Merseyside have been able to open their doors to the dying who are most in need of acceptance and love.

At the same time, the Aids pandemic, and its victims, challenge Christians to think through the meaning of the gospel. This virulent disease compels us to think more seriously than ever before, perhaps, about the dignity of the human person; sin and forgiveness; corporate and personal guilt; the meaning of redemption; and the Christian hope. As we have tried to face such issues, it has become patently clear that doctrinal and social ecumenism cannot be sundered. Moreover, if these two dimensions of our work need each other, so they also need to be integrated with the third member of the trio – spiritual ecumenism. Without the life of devotion, doctrine becomes arid and merely cerebral. Starved of the oxygen of prayer, social action may soon wilt and languish. Alternatively, it may harden into a brittle activism from which the joy of the Spirit has gone.

It is with this realm of sharing in spirituality that this book is chiefly concerned. It is partly a sharing of personal experience, not least the heady – I almost said intoxicating

– experience of working closely with fellow-Christians in Liverpool. I am drawing near to the end of my active ministry now, but I can truthfully say that for me, ecumenically speaking, the Lord of the feast has kept the best wine till last. In our Church Leaders' Group, we meet regularly for business and planning; but also for meals and relaxation, for friendship, conversation, laughter. Again, we meet for serious doctrinal discussion, when we try not to shirk the tough and divisive issues. Authority, priesthood and ministry, the ordination of women, the sacraments, the role of Mary in the Church: all these and more have commanded our frank discussion and debate. Alongside all these other activities, permeating them, and lifting them to a new dimension, is the life of prayer we share together.

Dr Olive Wyon, the Church of Scotland theologian, has stressed the importance of ecumenical encounters in prayer, not least in the small informal group. She gave examples of how people had been changed and mellowed by such experiences. For instance, a very stiff Anglo-Catholic of the old school, distinctly cold towards Free Church Christians, testified, 'I used to be a "spike", until I heard a Nonconformist pray; and then all my spikes fell off.' The Nonconformist, no doubt, prayed extempore, out of a long tradition of free prayer. That tradition can easily be debased, especially when no longer rooted in the simple dignity of biblical language, wedded to fresh and contemporary experience. Yet the Liverpool encounter has brought home sharply to me that the gift of extemporary prayer still flourishes, not only in the Free Churches, but also among Anglicans and Roman Catholics. It is as though their long schooling in the offices of liturgical prayer has given strength and sinew to the more personal offerings to God. Time was, when in mixed ecumenical company, an Anglican or Catholic would most readily reach for a collect or set form of prayer. Not any more, in an exclusive sense. They have found a new freedom, in which the collect is not spurned, but supplemented. I suspect one reason for the change is the subtle interchange which spiritual ecumenism has brought about. As the Free Churches have taken much more seriously the virtues of liturgical forms of prayer, so something of the Free Church pattern has been acquired by Catholics and Anglicans.

I believe there has begun a similar sharing and exchange in other areas of spirituality: in our hymn-singing traditions; in our understanding and practice of the Eucharist; in theology and experience of the Spirit; and in new forms of Christian community and belonging. There is a comprehensive agenda here, A good field and a large. The chapters that follow will attempt a little gleaning in it.[1]

3

EDWARD KING AND UNITY IN CHRIST

O N SUNDAY 19TH MAY, 1985, a special service of celebration took place in Lincoln Minster. The Dean and Chapter had planned it to commemorate the centenary of Edward King's coming into the diocese. He was Bishop of Lincoln from 1885 to 1910, the year of his death. Since he had died so long ago, few of those present in the cathedral that summer afternoon could recall him personally. It is true that the Alternative Service Book of the Church of England lists him in its Calendar of Saints – under 8th March, the day of his death, it records 'Edward King. Bishop of Lincoln, Teacher, Pastor'. Yet, in view of the lapse of time, there was genuine doubt as to whether the congregation would prove worthy of the occasion.

As we walked across the cathedral green for the service, the Chancellor, John Nurser, commented, only half in jest, 'We don't know if there's going to be anybody there, you know.' For a moment, I had a vision of the cathedral three-quarters empty. Perhaps the celebration should have been confined to the choir, rather than given over to the vast nave of the minster? We need not have been perturbed. When we entered the church, we were confronted with a great throng of worshippers – young and old, Anglicans, Catholics, Free Church people. There was a sense of joy and thanksgiving that was almost palpable. One of Edward King's favourite words was 'brightness'; and there was a special brightness in the faces of some very elderly people, in their eighties and nineties, who were sitting in the front few rows of pews. I asked who they were, and why they had been given these seats of honour. I was told that each of them had been confirmed as a child by Bishop King. That was why they were bursting with quiet pride and joy. A saint had laid his hands on them, and all through their long lives, his blessing had remained with them.

Who was Edward King? That was the question I asked myself when I first heard his name, having returned to my native Lincolnshire to my first pastoral appointment in 1961. It is a measure of how segregated traditions of spirituality could be, that, though born and bred in the county of Lincoln, I had hitherto lived in complete ignorance of this Anglican saint. I was first brought up against the tradition of Edward King when I stayed at the Old Palace, Lincoln, the house in which he had lived. Typically, he had declined to live in the great country residence occupied by his predecessors. He wanted to be accessible, near his cathedral, and close to his clergy and people. So he moved into the heart of the city, where he had the Old Palace, the much smaller medieval home of the bishops, restored, and set his pastoral motto above its entrance: '*Pascite gregem* – Feed the flock.'

In 1962, I happened to be staying in the Old Palace – Edward King House as it is called today – for a conference of Methodist ministers. On the staircase of the house I was mildly astonished to see a large engraving of an Anglican bishop being tried before an ecclesiastical court, presided over by E. W. Benson, the then Archbishop of Canterbury. The bishop was Edward King. He had been charged with liturgical offences, in contravention of the Book of Common Prayer, in what was to become the most celebrated ritual trial of the nineteenth century. In the Lincoln Judgement of Archbishop Benson, he was acquitted on most of the charges. He emerged as the most popular man in Lincolnshire, though at considerable cost to his health and peace of mind. The local people were convinced that the whole business 'broke him up a lot', and certainly, as we can see from his photographs, the experience aged him.

I went home from that Lincoln conference eager to find out more about Edward King, his life and character, and his career prior to his coming to Lincoln. I was encouraged in the search by my pastoral contacts with Lincolnshire people in Louth and its surrounding villages. Having seen the great engraving of his trial, I now found his portrait in many places. In pastoral visiting, I would find his photograph treasured in the homes of many people, not all of them Anglicans, or even members of any church. Lincolnshire people, certainly in the countryside, tend to be folk of few words until you get to know them well. They can indeed be rather 'clunch', to use a dialect word. They are not given to gushing or obvious hero-worship. They prize character and deeds far above words. 'It's all right talking . . .' is a phrase they often use, and it is not meant as a compliment.

Yet among these long-headed people, who can be rather dour, I found Edward King was a name to conjure with. They would kindle at the mere mention of him. After I had left Lincolnshire, and was teaching at Wesley College, Bristol, I embarked on research into the life and thought of Bishop King. I wanted to try to tap the stream of oral reminiscence which I knew was still available in the memories of the Lincolnshire people. Styling myself 'a Lincolnshire man in exile in the West Country', I wrote to the editor of *Lincolnshire Life*, the county journal, asking readers if they would share with me any personal reminiscences, oral or documentary, which they might have of Bishop King. For some six weeks after my letter appeared, I received a steady stream of replies giving vivid recollections of the life and character, the deeds and sayings of Bishop King. A few quotations from that postbag may give the flavour of their varied contents. One old lady wrote:

> Your letter reminded me of a remark that was repeated to me more than once as a child, by an aunt of mine . . . Bishop King decided to give up living at the Bishop's Palace out at Riseholme and to have his home in Lincoln because 'It wasn't every poor parson who had half-a-crown for a cab out to Riseholme.' These were the actual words that were repeated as his and always remained with me . . . I can remember as a child in

Lincoln what an aura there was about the name and person of Bishop King and these words always stuck vividly in my mind.'

Another lady, in her eighties, recalled how as a schoolgirl she had been scolded by her teacher for cutting across the cathedral green and through the minster, in haste to get to school. King heard about the telling-off, sought the child out, and, in the old lady's words, 'told me that whenever I wanted to do so, I could cross the green, and I remember his words – "It is my cathedral and my green, and you can go on them every day, if you want to do so." Now when I go to Lincoln, I purposely walk right across the cathedral green, and remember his kindness and love to his little ones.'

These sayings of Edward King, treasured by the people of his diocese, are typical of a whole tradition of the man. They match the way in which his portrait is kept, not only in the homes, but in the churches of Lincolnshire. All over the county, you may find his portrait in the churches which were once under his pastoral care. Photographs, engravings, water-colours – they are to be found in churches High, Low and middle-of-the-road in their worshipping traditions. In Louth, for example, one might expect to find his portrait in St Michael and All Angels, a High Church parish, sharing King's own Tractarian tradition. But it is also preserved in St James's, the great medieval parish church of the town; and, even more surprisingly, in Holy Trinity, a church with a pronounced Evangelical pattern of worship and piety. Needless to say, the Lincolnshire people do not make a habit of putting up their bishop's portrait in the churches. The truth is that Edward King was recognized as a saint, even in his lifetime; and his icons are treasured.

Having tapped into this living tradition of a Lincolnshire saint, I was drawn to find out more about the man. He was born on 29th December, 1829, and could remember the battle of Waterloo being talked of, during his childhood, as a recent event. Before he began his long episcopate at Lincoln, he had spent more than thirty years in and around Oxford. He studied as an undergraduate at Oriel College, where he was deeply influenced by one of the Fellows, Charles Marriott. As King said himself, 'If I have any good in me, I owe it to Charles Marriott. He was the most Gospel-like man I have ever met.'

After Oriel, King did some work as a private tutor, and then became curate in the parish of Wheatley, near Oxford, where again his portrait can be seen in the church. He was then appointed first as chaplain, then principal, of Cuddesdon College, just outside Oxford. In more recent times, the same post was held by Robert Runcie, who, like King, combined the principalship with the pastoral care of the parish. Cuddesdon, as a High Church foundation, was attacked as Romanizing, but to those who knew it best it was a place where holiness and happiness met together in a remarkable way. The quality of its community life was unforgettable to those who experienced it. Robert Milman, a somewhat hard-boiled ecclesiastic, could say of it, 'It was like a breath from the Garden of Eden before the door was shut.'[1]

After fifteen years at Cuddesdon, King was appointed as Professor of Pastoral Theology in the University of Oxford, and moved into residence as a Canon of Christ Church. In each of his varied spheres of work, King excelled as pastor and spiritual guide. His extraordinary gifts of sympathy, tact, shrewdness and insight were devoted to the human and spiritual needs of his people, whether these were country parishioners, Anglican ordinands, or members of the university. Indeed, Lord Elton, one of King's biographers and grandson of King's vicar at Wheatley, goes so far as to say that, 'During his twelve years in Oxford King became unquestionably the most powerful religious influence in the University.'[2]

That claim may seem exaggerated, if we equate religious influence with theological scholarship. Certainly, in the technical sense, King was no great theologian. At the same time, the idea that he was an intellectual lightweight, which some critics put about when he was made professor, is quite false. Any serious reading of King's writings will dispel that myth. E. C. Brightman, the great Anglican liturgiologist, who knew

King well, went so far as to put him 'among the most intellectual persons' he had known. Brightman glossed that view by
adding, 'only, as was perhaps the case with St Anselm, to
whom he has been compared, his intelligence was so much
a part of his character, so wholly himself, that it might easily
escape notice in the simplicity and charm of his personality.'
That is a recognizable, though rare type of character, and
many of King's contemporaries endorsed it as true of him.
Brightman rounds off his note by witnessing that King 'had
a singularly alert mind, and was interested in everything; no
one ever saw him bored, and he never touched a topic
without displaying an original view, and he was really alive
to the intellectual difficulties of his day. He knew and could
talk French, German, and Italian; and in a mixed company
he could talk in at least three languages at once – no mean
accomplishment; while his English was admirable, and he
read widely to the end.'[3]

It so happens that we can judge for ourselves the quality
of King's teaching, since a set of his lectures in pastoral
theology, given at Oxford in 1874, has survived. They were
published in 1932 by Eric Graham, then King's successor as
principal of Cuddesdon College. Graham took them from
the manuscript notebook of an old student of King's, Canon
Frewer of Brede in Sussex. Graham was convinced that
Edward King should rightly be numbered among the saints
of God, 'For what we find here is a life of supernatural
holiness and beauty, based firmly and explicitly on that 'full
Catholic faith' which he always claimed as our rightful heritage.' He goes on to apply to King the words of St James,
'The wisdom that is from above is first pure, then peaceable,
gentle, easy to be entreated, full of mercy and good fruits,
without variance, without hypocrisy.' Finally, Graham
endorses Brightman's tribute to King's intellectual and
moral power:

> It would be a mistake to suppose that Dr. King's influ-
> ence during his Oxford days was limited to the under-
> graduates. He had no strictly academic distinctions, but
> he had intellectual power of a high order, and he had

wisdom. So he was a force to be reckoned with among the senior members of the University. More especially he appealed to the younger dons who were adherents of the Oxford Movement; combining as he did the austerity of its first great champions with the more liberal outlook of the rising generation; and enriching both with a fragrant loveliness of character all his own.[4]

The pastoral lectures shed a great deal of light on Edward King, and on his ideal of Church and ministry. They soon dispel the myth that he was an unlearned man. They are replete with wide reading – in the Scriptures, the Early Fathers (Augustine, Chrysostom, Ambrose); the medieval Schoolmen (Aquinas, Lombard, Bonaventure); and the classic Anglican divines. He draws especially on the High Churchmen of the Tractarian tradition – Newman, Keble, Pusey, J. M. Neale. Yet the interesting impression that comes through his lectures is that King, though rooted in his own tradition, is not hidebound by it. In order to sew, we must have a knot in the thread, certainly; and King has that rooted commitment. At the same time, he has a breadth, a catholicity, and a human warmth that makes him open to Christian traditions very different from his own.

His openness and breadth of concern may be glimpsed in what he says to his ordinands about preaching. The preacher needs to know his Bible and the wealth of the Christian tradition; but he must also use every means to understand human nature. King advises:

> Read the poets ethically – e.g. Aeschylus, Dante, Homer, Shakespeare, Milton, Tennyson. Read good sermons, such as Newman's. Read thoughtfully; analyse them. Read good novels. You will thus travel into circumstances, and conditions, and situations of life. This knowledge of man must exist in order to apply the other knowledge. You may also learn much by a knowledge of yourself, but you must get a hold of human nature *somehow*.[5]

King himself was prepared to learn from the widest possible range of sources. Understandably, as a leading Anglo-Catholic, he was more than willing to learn from Roman Catholics, though he was by no means uncritical of what he called 'The Roman system'. The hard, centralized, authoritarian aspects of Rome were alien to him. That did not prevent him from loving Rome's worship and admiring her saints. What is more surprising, granted his churchmanship, is his readiness to learn from John Wesley and the Methodist people. He recognized here too a genuine tradition of Christian holiness, and was prepared to learn from it. When he was appointed to Lincoln as bishop, he knew he had no easy furrow to plough. The standard of the clergy left more than a little to be desired. One friend warned him that the clergy of the diocese of Lincoln were exhaustively divisible into three categories: those who were going out of their minds; those who had gone out of their minds; and those who had no minds to go out of! A gross exaggeration, of course, but one that had a grain of truth in it. So much so that King, with his long experience of training ordinands, took as one of his main pastoral aims the improvement of the standard of the clergy.

Another difficulty for the new bishop was that so many of the Christians in his diocese were not Anglicans. In this Methodist heartland almost every village had its chapel, often more than one, to accommodate the Wesleyan and Primitive brands of the Methodist movement. King's response to this challenge is interesting. Just before he went to Lincoln, he wrote to his friend, Robert Ottley, 'I am glad it is John Wesley's diocese. I shall try to be the Bishop of the poor.'[6] He may well have been thinking of the contemporary Lincolnshire Methodists, many of whom were poor farm labourers, and their families. Bishop King certainly wanted to reach out to them, and if possible draw them back into communion with the Church. Yet there was more to his aspiration than that. King knew Wesley's writings and the nature of his ministry. When he associated Wesley with his own desire to be a 'Bishop of the poor', he knew what he was doing. The very first open-air sermon John Wesley ever preached in England, was on the text Luke 4:18–19, which set the keynote of his whole ministry: 'The Spirit of the Lord is upon me because he has anointed me; he has sent me to announce good news to the poor, to proclaim release for prisoners and recovery of sight for the blind; to let the broken victims go free, to proclaim the year of the Lord's favour' (NEB).

That was the kind of ministry that King aspired to, and, in the event, fulfilled. Many Methodists were attracted by it. Not that they returned to the Church in droves, though they certainly went to hear King preach. His sermons were simple, direct, evangelical, practical. They reached parts of his hearers' hearts and minds that many other preachers could not touch. Wesley's sons and daughters, as they listened to him, said with a joyful surprise, 'He's nowt but an owd Methody.' Certainly King himself had a soft spot for the Methodist people, and a humble, penitent, ecumenical attitude towards them. As he wrote in 1906:

> I have never had any harsh feelings towards Nonconformists, and, I might add, especially not towards Wesleyans and Primitive Methodists, because I have always felt that it was the want of spiritual life in the Church and brotherly love which led them to separate. The more we draw near to Christ ourselves and fill ourselves with His Spirit, the greater power we shall have for unity. What we want is more *Christlike Christians*[7]

King wrote that in a private letter to a friend. Yet he was quite prepared publicly to acknowledge his debt to Wesley and the Methodist tradition. In his pastoral lectures at Oxford, stressing the need for the clergyman to be disciplined in self-examination, he draws on Wesley's early experiment with the 'bands', small, intimate groups, where mutual confession and support were practised: 'Wesley advised his band-meeting people to ask daily: (1) What have I done wrong? (2) What great temptations have I escaped? (3) What have I said or done of which I am not sure if it is sin or not?'[8] It must be rare for an Oxford High Churchman to know the Methodist tradition as well as King did, let alone to commend aspects of its practice as exemplary for Anglican priests in training. It is a measure of King's deeply ecumenical spirit that he did so quite naturally. He could be as critical of Nonconformity as he was of Roman Catholicism; but that did not prevent his learning from both, at the profoundest level of the things of the spirit.

4

A TALE OF TWO BISHOPS

IF EDWARD KING was sympathetic to the Methodists and their traditions of piety, he was certainly drawn to Roman Catholics. The Methodists he found close at hand, in his own diocese. The Catholics who influenced him most, however, were to be found mainly across the Channel, in continental Europe where his linguistic ability made him very much at home.

Henry Scott Holland, a fellow-canon of Christ Church, and a close friend of King, speaks about his 'rounded normality'. What Holland says about King's character, we might equally well apply to his ecumenism: 'There was nothing in him one-sided, or excessive, or unbalanced ... Everything hung together.'[1] When we look at his debt to Roman Catholic devotion, we see both his appreciation of the Catholic tradition and also his sturdy Anglican independence which could on occasion be critical of it.

It is not clear how far Bishop King made contact with Roman Catholics in England, and particularly in the diocese of Lincoln. What we do know is that, whenever he travelled abroad, in France, Germany, Switzerland, he would make a point of consulting the local Roman bishop, to compare notes about diocesan life, clergy training, and pastoral practice. We know too that he read with great appreciation some of the leading Roman Catholic divines of the Continent. He knew the writings of Dupanloup, the great educationist who was Bishop of Orleans from 1849 until his death in 1878. He also read Fénelon (1651–1715), the notable Archbishop of Cambrai, who was spiritual writer, mystic and eloquent preacher of the gospel to seventeenth-century France. Most of all, however, he drew on the voluminous works of J. M. Sailer (1751–1832), Bishop of Regensburg (Ratisbon), whose influence earned him the title of 'Patriarch of the Catholic Church in Bavaria.'[2]

Sailer is virtually unknown in Britain, though he is regarded as a towering figure on the Continent. His intellectual influence was matched only by his pastoral devotion and personal charm. It is easy to see why his character and writings should both have appealed to Edward King. They were spiritually blood-brothers, and even their outward careers have a striking similarity. Each was, in turn, principal of a theological seminary, professor of pastoral theology, and diocesan bishop. It may be that, with increasingly closer links between British and continental Christianity, Sailer may come into his own in this country. If so, Edward King will have prepared the way. Moreover, the traffic may develop in the reverse direction too, as German devotees of Sailer come to know of King. In 1968 a young German Benedictine, Augustine Pütz, had recently returned to his abbey after a spell of sabbatical leave in Cambridge. There, to his delight, he had discovered Edward King, and on his return to Germany published an article entitled 'Bishop Edward King, an Anglican friend of Sailer'. He writes with great discernment about King's episcopal ministry, and the pastoral and spiritual rapport between the two men. As Bishop of Lincoln, Pütz recognizes, King 'made it his "central idea", as Sailer would call it, to bring to the people, and especially to the poor, the blessings of the Church'.[3]

The same was true of Sailer. Both bishops were intellectuals and teachers yet neither had the slightest trace in his make-up of the remote and ineffectual don. On the contrary, each used direct and simple language, homely illustrations, and an imaginative sympathy that could see life through other people's eyes. Deep calls to deep. When King came to read Sailer, the book that attracted him most strongly was the German bishop's great three-volume *Lectures on Pastoral Theology*. King used it first for his teaching at Oxford, but the book is anything but academic in the pejorative sense. The *Lectures* are rooted in the soil of the Bavarian country-

side and its peasantry, and yet fully alive to the intellectual
challenges of the day.

Despite their differences in time and place and in social
background, King was naturally drawn to Sailer in a number
of ways. First, King had a real apostolate to the country poor,
which found ready expression at Wheatley, where he was
curate; at Cuddesdon, where he was vicar; and in Lincolnshire, where he was bishop. Sailer, for his part, was born and
bred in rural poverty in Bavaria. His father was a village
cobbler, with a large brood of children. Johann Michael had
no formal schooling until he was ten, when he was sent away
to be educated by the Jesuits in Munich. That was only
possible because of help from friends in the village, and for
a time it was touch and go whether the family could afford
the fees. It is a moving experience to gaze on Sailer's memorial in Regensburg Cathedral – which, incidentally, King
once made a special pilgrimage to see. Both men loved
children, and Sailer's statue is flanked by a small boy and
girl. The girl is holding his pastoral staff for him; the boy is
offering a book for Sailer to write in. To have children
present on a formal episcopal monument is unusual enough.
The discerning visitor may notice a further unlikely feature:
on either side of the memorial there is carved into the stone
a snipe. This brace of birds seems incongruous until we
learn the story behind them. For Sailer they were symbolic
of the overruling providence of God in his life.

When his father and a friend took the ten-year-old Sailer
on foot to Munich to start school, they had hopes of finding
him lodgings in a home where another boy from the village
was staying. Towards the end of the long journey, however,
the friend advised Sailer's father to take a present for the
prospective landlord, in case he should be reluctant to admit
another youthful boarder. All the father could afford was a
pair of snipe, which in the event opened the door to cheap
lodgings and enabled the boy to begin his outstanding
career as a scholar. In after years, as professor and bishop,
if he was ever served snipe at a meal, Sailer would tell fellow-
guests, 'Under God, I owe everything I have been enabled
to do to a pair of these birds!' Outstanding scholar that he

became, he never lost his passionate concern for the Christian formation of the poorest folk in the villages. Edward King shared the same commitment to be a 'bishop of the poor'.

The two men had something else in common, namely the close personal rapport they built up, as theological teachers, with the young men they were preparing for the priesthood. King had a most marked gift for getting alongside young men, for challenging them with the claims of Christ, and for attracting them to his service. Many who had gone up to Oxford without the slightest idea of ordination found themselves, to their astonishment, drawn to it through the influence of Edward King. Scott Holland records a typical instance, in his charming collection of letters to Mary Drew, Gladstone's daughter, *A Forty Years' Friendship*. He tells Mrs Drew of an encounter he had in 1883: 'I saw an "Angel" last night, a Mr —, from some living in Northamptonshire, beautiful, intelligent, thoughtful, charming... He knows men I think; rowed in his boat at Oxford; then got wholly snared by King.'[4]

Sailer had the same kind of relationship with the young men he taught in the German theological faculties. He chose to dedicate his *Pastoral Theology* to 'All who have lent ear, heart and spirit to his pastoral teaching in the universities of Dillingen and Ingolstadt-Landshut'. The lectures consist essentially of 'pastoral teaching', as King's did at Oxford; and Sailer's preface suggests how strong were the ties that bound him to his ordinands: 'Your names, your gifts, your progress, your deeds, are unforgettable to me; so is your love and the relationship in which we stand to one another.'[5]

A third reason why Sailer's writings appealed to King stems from the German scholar's creative engagement with the spirit of his age. The French Revolution broke out at almost exactly the mid-point of Sailer's life, and he experienced the full force of the Age of Reason and the philosophy of the Enlightenment. Sailer recognized the Enlightenment as a formidable challenge to the Catholic Church in Germany, and knew that it called for a concerted effort at theological and pastoral reconstruction. He urged his priests to

43

combat superstitious belief and practice – of which there was plenty in the Bavarian countryside – by means of clear Christian teaching drawn from the gospel. He was concerned to help raise up an educated clergy, well-read, versed in the new knowledge, and able to counter the arguments of unbelief.

In his essays on the formation of the Christian clergy, for example, he insists that they must have 'a life of the spirit, not simply the life of the mind'. Yet they must be educated men, who cultivate the life of the mind, and are at home in the realms of letters, art, science and society. Thus equipped, they will be able to have 'a special skill to work in the world . . . against the spirit of the world'. We see Sailer dealing with this theme in a powerful sermon he preached at the first Mass of one of his students, Father Schwabe. He takes as his theme 'The young clergyman of the nineteenth century' – topical both because of Schwabe's youth and because the year is 1801. He sets out the challenge the new age makes to the priest, and argues:

> The clergyman of the nineteenth century must know more, must be willing to do more, must be able to suffer more than a clergyman in other ages had to know, do, suffer. He must know more, since reflection, research, writing, living questions and answers in respect of Christianity, have in our days become more general than they once were; since general press freedom and popular freedom of travel, brings opinions for and against the Gospel more quickly into circulation than formerly was the case; since also, what was hitherto undoubted and uncontested, is now brought publicly into doubt and conflict . . . [6]

Yet Sailer is clear that the priest must, above all, be a Spirit-filled man, steeped in prayer, committed to Christ and his people.

Edward King had the same objective, both as pastoral professor and diocesan bishop. Since, however, Sailer died in 1832, when King was a mere infant, it may well be asked how and why a Catholic bishop, born in mid-eighteenth-century Bavaria, could speak so powerfully to an Anglican whose closing years coincided with the first decade of the twentieth century. The answer is twofold. First, Sailer was in many ways ahead of his age, in thought and practice. Indeed, modern Catholic theologians like Hans Küng (in *The Church*), see Sailer as one of the forerunners of the dynamic, biblical and ecumenical theology of the Second Vatican Council.[7] Sailer's ecumenical sympathies gave him a wide circle of Protestant friends and correspondents, and caused him trouble from time to time with the Vatican. Secondly, to understand Sailer's relevance for King, we must bear in mind the fact that there has often been a time-lag before German theology, breaking new ground, has made its impact on Britain.

Certainly King believed that, in the Oxford of the 1860s and 1870s, and more widely in late Victorian society, he was confronted by the same forces of rationalism, materialism and unbelief that Sailer had had to face some seventy-five years earlier. King spent the long vacation of 1875 in Germany, learning the language. He brought back with him to Oxford, as he began the Michaelmas term, a vivid impression of triumphant material progress in Germany. Yet with the rise of prosperity, he noted a drastic decline in piety:

It is very interesting seeing the wonderful upgrowth and power of the German nation; but the unbelief is very sad – only three per cent, they say, go to any sort of church in Berlin, and unbelief is quite open. They seem to have passed through the stages of Rationalism and Pantheism, and now they have almost ceased to care about the metaphysics which we have been following, and worshipping in them, and they are devoting themselves to physics. This means, I fear, for many, materialism. Ludthard says this plainly, meaning by materialism love of money or power or pleasure; this seems to be the leading danger now – that people will try to be respectable, but without God; to separate morality from religion, to devote themselves to civilisation and culture, and forget God.[8]

The notes that Sailer was sounding in 1801 at the induction of a young priest to a country cure in Bavaria, can be heard in a sermon which Edward King preached at Lincoln in 1907. He was dedicating a new chapel for the Bishop's Hostel, the diocesan theological college, in which he had taken such a strong personal interest. Like Sailer, King wants to see faith and knowledge integrated in the ministerial life. Like Sailer, he warns of the contemporary danger of making idols out of knowledge, power, and money. 'While I would encourage the instruction of candidates for Holy Orders in as many branches of knowledge as possible,' he says, 'our paramount duty at the present time seems to me to be the maintenance of the true end and object of knowledge. Money and what money will bring is the practical object of at least a large part of the knowledge of the present day . . .' It all sounds depressingly familiar, from a late twentieth-century perspective. Then King turns to religion and science:

> The increased knowledge of natural science ought to lead us to deeper love and reverence for the power and tenderness of God. The awful power and exactness with which the laws of nature work ought to lead us to more holy fear in our relation to the moral government of the world; but modern knowledge, the knowledge which is in such demand at the present day, is in great danger of being divorced from the knowledge and love of God.

King concludes that his contemporaries are 'in danger now of becoming entangled in the veil of a knowledge divorced from faith. They do well to acquire knowledge, but they ought to remember to look beyond and above.'[9] That was a constant theme of King's letters and sermons, and it seems clear that he was strengthened in his concern by what he learned from Bishop Sailer and the experience of the Church in Germany.

King and Sailer, then, shared a number of key concerns. Both wanted to bring the gospel to the poor, and to minister to their total need, material and spiritual. Both were committed to the search for deeper Christian unity. Both gave a large part of their ministry to theological training, and were committed to improving the quality of the clergy, to match the demands of a new age. Both saw clearly the challenge of modern unbelief and materialism, and strove for a convincing Christian apologetic. Finally, they shared a common approach to spirituality, doctrine and pastoral care. There is in the two men a similar blend of heart and head, of concern for doctrine and pastoral warmth, of devotion and shrewd common sense.

Take, for example, ministry to the sick, to which both bishops gave a high priority. Sailer compiled a *Little Bible for the Sick*, consisting of select biblical passages, prayers and meditations, sensitively chosen to suit the needs of the person afflicted with illness. King for his part was patron of the Guild of St Barnabas, formed in 1876 to provide fellowship and support for 'all trained nurses belonging to the Church who wish to make their service to the sick a service to the Lord Jesus Christ'. It had its own rule of life, and sponsored retreats and meetings both devotional and social. It published a monthly paper, *Misericordia*, to which King regularly contributed; and took as its motto the words of the great French surgeon, Ambroise Paré, 'I tended him; God cured him'. King was patron of the Guild from 1888 until his death twenty-two years later. Francis Russell, chaplain to the Guild, published in 1910 a collection of Bishop King's letters and addresses to the Guild members, entitled *Counsels to Nurses*. In his preface, he acknowledges the debt in spirituality which King owed to Sailer:

> Amongst the spiritual writers who most appealed to him, his favourite was, perhaps, Bishop Sailer of Ratisbon. He often quoted him to us and encouraged us to translate and print in *Misericordia* his writings. The two Bishops had indeed much in common, the same evangelical simplicity, the same warmth and tenderness of piety, the same all-embracing sympathy.[10]

Russell's judgement is confirmed by the series of Annual Letters which King wrote to the nurses of the Guild. At Christmas 1891, he tells them:

I am very glad to see this year that our good chaplain has introduced you to the mind and heart of Bishop Sailer, the 'German Fénelon', as he so well calls him. Bishop Sailer was a man with a real heart and mind: he lived at a time when many minds and hearts were troubled with unbelief, and with the social and personal miseries which go with it; and he tried in all ways he could to relieve the suffering in the minds and hearts of men. He was a sort of genius. He not only had some knowledge, but his mind saw the relation of things – how one thing touches another, around, below, and above: and so his mind has that kind of freshness, and strength, and gentleness, and simplicity, and depth, which follow from being in conscious touch with the circle of the One Truth.[11]

A year later, he recurs to this same theme:

I am glad to see that your good chaplain has more than fulfilled my hope that you might know something more of the mind of Sailer, the good Bishop of Regensburg. Let me remind you of three characteristics of his writings – simplicity, depth, repetition; and of three of his favourite words – light, life, and love; and repeat his words quoted in the January Paper for 1892 . . . 'That mankind fallen from God may receive again a mind, heart, and spirit for God, and become one, and remain one with Him for ever. This is the task, and final aim, of the whole Christian Church'.[12]

In 1903, the members of the Guild presented Bishop King with an original portrait of Sailer, which he was to keep for the rest of his life in his study at Lincoln, mounted on a special easel, a tangible reminder of his debt to Sailer's life and thought. In thanking them for the gift, he writes:

I never thought I should possess a real picture of dear Bishop Sailer, though I once went all the way to Regensburg to see his statue, and the place where he lived. I shall indeed value your gift exceedingly, and I hope that its presence in my room may help me to preserve, better than I have done, that spirit of inward piety, which is so easily crusted over, or crushed by the routine of hard work.[13]

It is difficult to assess just how much King owed to Sailer's life and thought. We have seen, for example, that both bishops set considerable store by ministry to the sick. In addition to the *Little Bible for the Sick*, Sailer devoted a major section of his *Lectures on Pastoral Theology* to this area of ministry. He heads his treatment of the theme with a word of Christ from Matthew 25, 'I was sick, and you visited me.' That text not only gives dominical warrant for ministering to the sick but, more profoundly, encourages the pastor to see in the sick person Christ himself. He speaks of the pastor as a mediator of Christ's presence to the sick person, adding, 'It is not the pastor as a human being who unites the sick person to God in Christ; rather, it is God in Christ who, through the pastor, awakens and strengthens eternal life in the one who is sick.' Then, combined with this high theology of the ministerial office, comes Sailer's characteristic and homely common sense, as he gives practical advice to the priest in the sickroom:

> Try to see that the air in the sick-room is fresh. Avoid breathing the infected breath of the sick person, in nose and mouth. As soon as he gets home [the pastor] changes his linen, and washes face, mouth and hands with vinegar and clean water . . . Have breakfast before making an early morning sick visit.[14]

It is interesting to compare Sailer's practical hints with those King gave to his Oxford students in his pastoral lectures of 1874. Dealing with pastoral visits in cases of infection, he counsels:

> Go everywhere and fearlessly, but observing these simple rules: (1) A golden rule. Don't go tired or fasting . . . Go after eating. Go when you are strong. (2) Don't stand between the sick bed and the fireplace because of the draught. (3) Don't hang over the bed,

or hold the sick man's hand. If he holds out his hand, tell him kindly that he must keep it covered up.[15]

We find in King as in Sailer a pastoral theology which comprehends as part of Christian ministry, humanity, kindness and good sense. These qualities shine out in Sailer's warning to his ordinands against wrong attitudes in the sickroom. The pastor mistakes his calling if he displays a great deal of book-learning, 'instead of speaking to the sick person a word that strikes home to his heart'. He fails again if he either arouses false expectations of recovery, or takes away all hope of life. He is wrong too if he preaches at the sick person, or speaks in a loud, strident tone, 'where he should let fall, in soft, gentle tones, a word here and there of comfort and instruction.'[16]

Finally, in their ministry to the dying, the two bishops exemplify a theology of grace which is available even, or rather especially, to those who have done great wrong and are about to suffer for it. Sailer in his *Lectures on Pastoral Theology* devotes a long section to the needs of a prisoner condemned at law and awaiting execution. That was precisely the situation that confronted Bishop King in 1887, when he ministered in Lincoln jail to a young Grimsby fisherman who had been condemned to death for killing his sweetheart in a lover's quarrel. King spent long hours in the death-cell with him, and told him in his own words the story of the Prodigal Son, whom the father forgave and welcomed home. The boy from Grimsby had no religious background, and little moral sense. Indeed some contemporaries pronounced him hardly more than a powerful animal. Yet under King's ministry, God's grace touched the depths of his being, and he was profoundly converted to faith in Christ. King confirmed him and gave him his first, and last, Communion in the death-cell. He met his end with great courage and calmness of spirit. King went with him to the scaffold and ministered to him until the end. Afterwards, he wrote to a friend, 'It was a terrible privilege, but I am most thankful that I was allowed to be with the poor dear man . . . his last (and first) Communion on Sunday morning put me to shame. I felt quite unworthy of him. How little the world knows of the inner life.'[17]

King's attitude and practice in this most testing area of pastoral care were fully in accord with Sailer's teaching, which King had known, through the *Lectures on Pastoral Theology*, since his Oxford days. Sailer sets out a theology of grace which is able to change the worst of men into a disciple of Christ, and which will despair of no single human soul. He assures the pastor that 'there is no crime so great that God cannot forgive, and which the Spirit of Christ cannot cancel.' A Methodist is reminded of Charles Wesley's claim that 'the vilest offender may turn and find grace.' Indeed, Sailer's words breathe an Evangelical Arminianism which the Wesleys would readily have owned: 'God wants to make all sinners holy, Christ has died for all, the Spirit of God knocks at every heart.' Moreover, Sailer gives detailed practical advice on how to minister to a person under condemnation of death:

> In the last three hours before execution, the pastor will no longer leave the condemned man on his own, but will strengthen him with prayers before he treads the heavy road to death, and then also, with brief expressions, all leading him to God in Christ and to a blessed eternity, will accompany him, first, to the court house, where sentence of death on him will be formally pronounced before the people, and afterwards to the scaffold.[18]

It was exactly in that spirit that Edward King dealt with the lad from Grimsby.

In all these ways, the Catholic Bishop Sailer and the Anglican Bishop King were kindred spirits. Deep called to deep, across the years that separated them, and across the denominational divide. It is no mere antiquarianism to recall their lives and teaching. They speak to us from within the Communion of Saints, and we are better for knowing them. More than that, as the 1990s open up a vista of closer economic and political ties among the European peoples, they remind us of the wealth of Christian spirituality there is to explore

51

across the Channel. I found this prospect one to ponder during a month's research on the King-Sailer axis in the archives at Regensburg. That bishopric was in fact founded by an Englishman – Boniface of Crediton, the apostle of Germany. Also in Bavaria I encountered the Mary Ward Sisters, founded by that remarkable seventeenth-century Yorkshirewoman. Her order of nuns is responsible for a series of fine schools for girls, and its members are still known in Germany as 'The English Sisters'. Moreover, within the walls of medieval Regensburg stands the Church of St Jakob (St James) still known as the 'Scottish Church'. Founded by Irish monks, it was later taken over by the Scottish Benedictines, and it is moving to read the great series of Latin memorial tablets to former abbots. These men, who gave their lives to the Church in Germany, bear classic Scots names like Robert Scott and John Leith. Today the church, still a lively centre of worship, is the chapel of the diocesan seminary.

The diocese needs a large seminary chapel, for, as Bishop Manfred Müller told me, it has 1200 secular priests and 200 more in the orders. Interestingly, the bishop is a convinced Anglophile, with a superb command of the Queen's English. I had prepared a few sentences of greeting from the Liverpool church leaders, and delivered them to him in my halting German. With supreme tact, he replied, 'If you don't mind, I should prefer to speak your language. You see, I like to practise my English. I could do with you to correct my pronunciation.' I assured him he had no such need; to which he replied casually, 'Well, you see, I was a prisoner-of-war in Cumberland from 1945 to 1946.' He had been well treated by the country people as he worked on a Cumbrian farm, and had not forgotten. Hence, in one sense, his excellent English, which he had kept up, as he had his friendships and contacts with British people. I could only wish that my German had been able to match his English. Bishop King's would have done, had he been able to talk with Bishop Sailer's successor. In our exploration of continental Christianity, we may be just beginning to catch up with Edward King.

5

THE HEART STRANGELY WARMED:
A METHODIST RESPONSE TO
ORTHODOXY

IN 1950, THE French Roman Catholic writer, Julien Green, was on a visit to London. As usual on his travels, he kept a journal, and the entry for 18th December registers his blank amazement at coming across an unusual plaque in the City of London. What astonished him was this extremely public way of commemorating what was a very personal religious experience. 'I find it strange', he records 'that in London, in Aldersgate Street, there should be on a bank the following inscription: "It is probably in a house on this site that, on the 24th May 1738, John Wesley felt his heart 'strangely warmed'." '

The reference is, of course, to the most celebrated entry in John Wesley's own *Journal*, where he writes under this date:

> I went very unwillingly to a society in Aldersgate Street, where one was reading Luther's Preface to the Epistle to the Romans. About a quarter before nine, while he was describing the change which God works in the heart through faith in Christ, I felt my heart strangely warmed. I felt I did trust in Christ, Christ alone, for salvation, and an assurance was given me that he had taken away *my* sins, even *mine*, and saved *me* from the law of sin and death.[1]

Methodists, who annually celebrate 24th May as the anniversary of a major turning point in Wesley's life and ministry, might see nothing unusual in the tablet on the wall of

53

Barclay's Bank. Green, however, could hardly believe his eyes, and his kindled imagination led him to speculate about the possibility of finding such a memorial in the streets of Paris. Wesley's 'heart-warming' prompted thoughts of Pascal's spiritual enlightenment, his 'definitive conversion', when he discovered the 'God of Abraham, the God of Isaac, the God of Jacob, and not of the philosophers and men of science'. Like Wesley, Pascal wrote down his experience. Moreover, the Frenchman sewed the paper into his doublet, and carried it on his person for the rest of his life. Green imagines a visitor to Paris encountering a Pascal plaque on the lines of the Wesley one. He begins to fantasize: 'Just imagine a plaque telling us that on such and such a spot, on the 23rd of November, in the year of grace 1654, from half-past ten until about half-past midnight, Blaise Pascal . . .' Then the sheer incongruity of his musing breaks in upon him: 'No, I cannot imagine it'; but he adds, 'And yet perhaps those are the greatest events in the world'.[2]

Both Pascal and Wesley struggled to put into words their profound personal encounters with the living God. In describing their Christian experience, both men use the term 'heart'. Alongside Pascal's 'The heart has its reasons which reason knows nothing of', we may put Wesley's 'I felt my heart strangely warmed'. Are they simply retreating into an irrational emotionalism? I think not. Both were highly rational men: Pascal a brilliant mathematician, Wesley a master of logic in the Oxford schools, who addressed so many of his 'Appeals' to 'Men of Reason and Religion'. In speaking of the 'heart', neither one of them is disparaging the light of human reason. To understand them, we need to grasp the profound biblical meaning of the 'heart', as the central core of the human person.

The term 'heart' in modern speech has become almost as debased as the word 'love'. Yet 'heart', for both the Orthodox and the Methodist traditions, is of seminal importance. Orthodox Christians speak of 'prayer of the heart', as prayer which involves the whole person and permeates the whole pattern of living. This rich tradition of Orthodox devotion was brought home to me afresh by reading Constance

Babington Smith's life of *Iulia de Beausobre: A Russian Christian in the West.* Iulia de Beausobre writes, in a note of 24th November 1960, of a constant, uninterrupted, wordless prayer, which flows on and on, as a deep undertow within the stream of the believer's life: 'Eventually prayer is wordless – it must be. The prayer without words means praying while talking, eating, driving, anything. The word "stream" in English and the Russian "*stremlenie*" convey something of it.'[3] Orthodox writers often speak of such prayer as praying with the 'mind in the heart'. The repeating of the 'Jesus prayer' (Lord Jesus Christ, Son of God, have mercy on me), until it becomes part of the rhythm of breathing, reminds us that 'prayer of the heart' involves the body too.

This Orthodox understanding of 'heart' derives ultimately from Scripture, where 'heart' does not signify simply feeling or emotion. It connotes the unity of the essential person – intellect, feeling, will – whom God calls and addresses. We have here, I believe, a link between Orthodox and Methodist devotion. Charles Wesley's hymns, which form the marrow of classical Methodist piety, have been described as 'the Scriptures in solution'. They abound in quotations, echoes, allusions from the biblical writers. Wesley does not use Scripture in any wooden, or scissors-and-paste way, as in some of the less inspired versions of the metrical Psalms. He blends biblical language, imagery and motifs in a most subtle and creative fashion. For Wesley, as Canon A. M. Allchin has rightly pointed out, 'heart' still retains its basically 'biblical and patristic meaning, as the centre of man's thinking and willing, as well as his feeling'.[4] It has not been diluted and distorted to mean merely the emotions, as in the words of the mythical curate to his congregation: 'I feel I have a feeling, and I feel you feel it too.'

Take, for example, Charles Wesley's great hymn on prayer which begins:

> Jesu, thou sovereign Lord of all,
>   The same through one eternal day,
> Attend thy feeblest followers' call,
>   And Oh! instruct us how to pray!

In the second verse, Wesley pleads for the Spirit of Jesus, that he may breathe his power into the hearts of his praying followers. It is quite clear in these lines that for Wesley 'heart' embraces will and intellect as well as feeling:

> We cannot think a gracious thought,
> We cannot feel a good desire,
> Till thou, who call'dst a world from naught
> The power into our hearts inspire.[5]

It is not only in the context of prayer that this emphasis on the heart is found in Wesley. It runs through the whole gamut of Methodist theology and devotion, and it connotes without question the central core of the person. The 'heart' is here the kernel or marrow of the whole human being, not just one isolated aspect of human nature. When the lover confesses to the beloved, 'I give you my heart,' he means not merely his feelings, but his whole person, his total life and love. So too for Wesley the heart and its consecration involves a complete self-surrender to God. This meaning is transparent in another hymn of Charles Wesley, which opens with an invocation to the Holy Spirit:

> Come, Holy Ghost, all-quick'ning fire!
> Come, and my hallowed heart inspire . . .

The hymn concludes with a prayer of dedication and self-offering, whose final couplet speaks powerfully of the all-embracing significance of the heart:

> My will be swallowed up in thee;
> Light in thy light still may I see,
> Beholding thee with open face:
> Called the full power of faith to prove,
> Let all my hallowed heart be love,
> And all my spotless life be praise.[6]

Perhaps the clearest example of this inclusive, all-embracing sense of the heart in Wesley, is to be found in the fourth

verse of his noble Trinitarian hymn, 'Father, Son, and Holy
Ghost,/One in Three, and Three in One'. Here Wesley
invites the believer to offer up all his or her various powers
and faculties to the Triune God, and subsumes them all
under the term which for him signifies the whole person,
the heart:

> Take my soul and body's powers;
>   Take my memory, mind, and will;
> All my goods, and all my hours,
>   All I know, and all I feel!
> All I think, or speak, or do;
>   Take my heart: but make it new![7]

This stress on the whole person leads naturally to another
Methodist emphasis which may form a bridge to Orthodoxy,
namely the concern for holiness, Christian Perfection, or
'being made perfect in love'. For John Wesley, the doctrine
of Christian Perfection was 'the grand depositum which
God has lodged with the people called Methodists',[8] and he
preached it in season and out of season. In his judgement,
God had raised up the Methodists 'to spread scriptural holiness throughout the land'; and it was the quest for guides
to help his people along the road to sanctification that drew
him both to the Catholic mystics, and to Gregory of Nyssa,
the fountain-head of Orthodox monastic spirituality.

What did Wesley mean by holiness? Sadly, it has been one
of the most abused words in the Christian vocabulary. It
tends to provoke wary suspicion, if not downright revulsion.
One can well understand why, looking at some of the holiness cults that have used it as their brand name or house
style. In the early 1970s, when I was teaching in the Methodist college in Bristol, I preached at a joint Anglican-
Methodist harvest festival in a Gloucestershire village. The
vicar conducted the service, which was in the parish church,
and invited me over to the vicarage for coffee afterwards. It
transpired that his mother was a member of the Plymouth
Brethren, indeed of the strictest section of the movement,
the Closed Brethren. A few years previously, the Closed

Brethren in England had been plunged into anguished debate by a dictate of Big Jim Taylor, so-called, the world-wide leader of the community. He had issued a stern order, which brooked no exception, that from now on, no member of the Closed Brethren was to hold table fellowship, that is, eat a meal, with any non-member. It mattered not that the non-member might be the member's wife, husband, son or daughter. Henceforth, it was to be separate tables. The vicar and his family realized something was seriously awry when Granny, who had always been the soul of hospitality, started to make excuses as to why she could not offer them a meal. 'Let's have a sandwich in the car,' became a standard ploy. Eventually the truth came out, and they came to understand that they had Big Jim Taylor to thank for this division in their family life.

Their family distress was mirrored in many other homes. A Member of Parliament sought to have Taylor barred from entering the country, since his words and actions were having such a disruptive effect on people's lives. Husbands were set against wives, parents against children. There were even isolated cases of suicide. Taylor, however, defended himself vigorously and was quite unrepentant. In reply to the MP who sought to ban him from Britain, he published an Open Letter justifying his stance from Scripture. The vicar who was recalling all these events to me had a copy of the letter, and asked my opinion of it. I read it carefully, and found it full of select quotations from St Paul's Second Letter to the Corinthians: 'What fellowship has light with darkness? . . . Come ye out from among them, and be ye separate, says the Lord . . . Do not be unequally yoked with unbelievers.'[9] And more to the like effect. 'What do you think of it?' the vicar asked me. 'It's the most extraordinary document of its kind I've read,' I told him. 'In one sense, he proves his case up to the hilt; but there is not one single mention of the name of Jesus of Nazareth, who ate and drank with publicans and sinners!'

That was one understanding of what it meant to be a holy people. Jealously guard your purity, and keep yourself strictly apart from those who do not belong to the select band. It is that kind of thinking and practice which has given 'holiness' a bad name. As a Methodist colleague once said to me, 'The trouble with so much of this talk about holiness is, that we're apt to be continually looking at our own white garments, with a sidelong glance at our neighbour's, as if to say, "Somebody's not using holiness." Wesley tried to guard against all such departures from the way of Jesus, whose critics could not stomach the fact that 'This man receives sinners and eats with them.'

What were Wesley's safeguards against bigotry and fanaticism? The text just quoted from the Gospels underlines the sovereign resource Wesley found in Scripture itself. He characteristically spoke to his people about 'Scriptural Holiness', and was really not interested in any other kind. He would cite the great call to the people of God in the Old Testament: 'You shall be holy; for I the Lord your God am holy' (Leviticus 19:2 RSV). To give content to that holiness, he went to the gospels, and centred on the words of Jesus: 'You shall love the Lord your God with all your heart, and with all your soul, and with all your strength, and with all your mind; and your neighbour as yourself' (Luke 10:27 RSV). One of Wesley's favourite summaries of the meaning of the Christian life was drawn from St Paul. In Galatians 5:6, Paul sums up Christian living as, essentially, 'faith working by love'. For Wesley, Christ-like love is the sovereign test of the genuineness of faith, and the heart of what he means by holiness. In his own words, 'Faith working by love is the length and breadth and depth and height of Christian perfection.'[10]

It is here that Methodist spirituality sets up a striking resonance with Orthodox devotion and its understanding of *sobornost*. *Sobornost*, the holy fellowship, or in Charles Williams's great phrase 'the coinherence', speaks of the closest solidarity in Christ, and rules out any individualistic approach to holiness. As Symeon Lash expresses it: 'Orthodox spirituality is not individualistic, since the Christian by his baptism has become a member of the body of Christ and it is as a member of that body that he advances on the road to deification.' Lash goes on to cite the great Russian theologian, Alexis Khomiakov, to reinforce the point: 'No one is saved alone, he is saved in the Church, as a member of it and in union with all its other members.'[11] Wesley could not have agreed more. He states uncompromisingly: 'The Gospel of Christ knows of no religion, but social; no holiness but social holiness.'[12] For him Christian holiness can never be some kind of individualized soul-culture, since it is social by its very nature. Hence he provides for his people a whole network of groups – bands, classes, societies – for fellowship, mutual care and upbuilding, for 'watching over one another in love'.

For Wesley, then, the essence of holiness is Christ-like love, humbly and practically expressed in the small change of daily living. The heart of it all, as he tirelessly explains, is simply more and more of that love which Paul describes in 1 Corinthians 13. It is to have 'the mind that was in Christ', and to walk as he walked. In his *Plain Account of Christian Perfection* there is a striking passage, written in the heat of a tumultuous revival movement, which brings it all down to earth. It also, incidentally, shows up so many modern holiness cults for the shoddy and unbiblical caricatures they are. Wesley urges his Methodist people:

> It were well you should be thoroughly sensible of this – the heaven of heavens is love. There is nothing higher in religion – there is, in effect, nothing else; if you look for anything but more love, you are looking wide of the mark, you are getting out of the royal way. And when you are asking others, 'Have you received this or that blessing?' if you mean anything but more love, you mean wrong; you are leading them out of the way, and putting them upon a false scent.[13]

So for John Wesley holiness means sharing in the *agape* of Christ, humble, gentle, patient love. Its test is not speaking in tongues, or the attainment of a set level on a Richter scale of religious emotion, but Christ-like character and the test of fruits. His brother Charles transposes the same sentiment into verse:

Thus may I show thy Spirit within,
  Which purges me from every stain;
Unspotted from the world and sin
  My faith's integrity maintain,
The truth of my religion prove
By perfect purity and love.[14]

This transformation of human nature by the Spirit of
God may appear at first sight very different from Orthodox
language about the 'deification' of the Christian. In fact,
though the language may be different, the thought is by no
means alien to Methodist spirituality. Certainly Wesley was
thoroughly familiar with the understanding that, as God in
Christ took upon him our human nature, so we, through
Christ, may rise to share the life of God.

A seminal text for Wesley on this theme was 2 Peter 1:4,
'Thus he has given us . . . his precious and very great promises, so that through them you may escape from
corruption . . . and may become participants of the divine
nature (NRSV). In his *Explanatory Notes upon the New Testament*,
John Wesley explains what he understands by this text,
namely, 'Being renewed in the image of God, and having
communion with Him, so as to dwell in God and God in
you.'[15]

Charles Wesley, in his hymns, draws on the same biblical
well. It is significant that, in the latest Methodist Hymn Book,
Hymns and Psalms, the textual index lists no fewer than nine
hymns which draw on this crucial passage from 2 Peter. A
few examples must suffice. In the great hymn of the Incarnation, 'Let earth and heaven combine', Charles has a verse
which extols the bridging of the chasm between divine and
human nature in Christ:

He deigns in flesh to appear
  Widest extremes to join;
To bring our vileness near,
  And make us all divine:
And we the life of God shall know,
For God is manifest below.[16]

In 'Father of everlasting grace', a hymn which is a prayer for the sending of the Spirit, the second verse reads:

> Send us the Spirit of thy Son,
> To make the depths of Godhead known,
>   To make us share the life divine;
> Send him the sprinkled blood to apply,
> Send him our souls to sanctify,
>   And show and seal us ever thine.[17]

Finally, one of Wesley's best known hymns opens with the plea that we may become what we are, by sharing the divine nature in Christ:

> Christ, from whom all blessings flow,
> Perfecting the saints below,
> Hear us, who thy nature share,
> Who thy mystic body are.[18]

Within the Methodist tradition, this call to holiness, with its sharing of the divine nature, comes to all the members of the Body. All are called to be saints. Wesley continually urged the solidarity of those who are in Christ, so that it became proverbial that 'the Methodists go to heaven in companies'. The context of many of the early Methodist hymns was not simply that of congregational worship. They were also designed to be sung within the class-meeting, the house fellowship, the small gathering in which Christians could build one another up in faith and love. Such, for instance, is Charles Wesley's hymn on 'The Communion of Saints', just cited, which continues:

> Closer knit to thee our Head,
> Nourish us, O Christ, and feed!
> Let us daily growth receive,
> More and more in Jesus live.

The small fellowship group fulfilled many purposes. It was the basic unit of pastoral care in Methodism, and the class leader was appointed as a sub-pastor to watch over and encourage his or her members. The meeting was also a school of prayer, where personal concerns and the needs of the neighbourhood could be offered to God. It was not least a place where each member could be encouraged to stir up the gift which God had given and find his or her own office and ministry within the life of the Christian community. The hymn we are considering goes on to implore God to:

> Move, and actuate, and guide,
> Divers gifts to each divide;
> Placed according to thy will,
> Let us all our work fulfil
>
> Never from our office move,
> Needful to each other prove;
> Use the grace on each bestowed,
> Tempered by the art of God.[19]

From this piety there came abundant offers of lay service and ministry – stewards, class leaders, local (lay) preachers – without whom Methodism could not, and cannot, function. Here too, then, we may discern some affinity between the Methodist and Orthodox traditions. Orthodoxy, for all its emphasis on the ordained priesthood, has also cherished the service of lay people. It has recognized the sovereign right of the Spirit to bestow his gifts as and where he will. So there are within the Orthodox churches lay spiritual guides (*startsi*), lay preachers, lay theologians. It is only in this last category that Methodism can scarcely bear comparison with Orthodoxy. There have not been many lay theologians in the Methodist tradition. A. S. Peake and Victor Murray have been rather the exception than the norm. In Orthodoxy, on the other hand, lay theologians are plentiful. Their calibre is often formidable. I recall an unforgettable encounter with Professor Nikos Nissiotis at the Montreal Faith and Order Conference of 1963, when we met in a small sub-group which was roughly the size of a Methodist class-meeting – about a dozen or so. It was memorable to be told by him: 'I do not say to you, Give up your Methodism in order to find Orthodoxy; I say rather find Orthodoxy *through your Methodism.*'

Still in the realm of lay piety and devotion, Methodism, like Orthodoxy, has its tradition of 'holy fools'. These men and women saw themselves, in St Paul's phrase, as 'fools for Christ's sake'. They often combined an exuberant joy with marked eccentricity and unusual prophetic insight. Such was Billy Bray (1794–1868), the converted Cornish tin-miner, who was known as 'The King's son'. 'I am the son of a King,' he claimed, because he had been brought into the adopted family of the sons and daughters of the Lord who was the King of glory. His conversion was dramatic, for he had been notorious as a drunkard and womanizer who mocked at religion with wit and panache. After his change, he emphatically did not become a model of decorum and respectability. His Celtic fire and overpowering joy found expression in his Methodist preaching, certainly. But it also broke out into singing and dancing, in which he was quite irrepressible. He would punctuate his walk to work with a series of leaps, and at each one shout 'Glory!' or 'Hallelujah!'. Even underground in the mine, 250 fathoms below ground, he could not be curbed. He said in retrospect, 'I could leap and dance for joy just as well underground as on the surface.' His workmates reasoned with him to contain his exuberance, but to no avail. 'My companions used to tell me that was no kind of religion – dancing, and singing and making so much to-do. But I was born in the fire and I couldn't live in the smoke!' His small stature enabled him to leap even under the low ceiling of the mineshaft.

> They said there was no need to leap and dance and make so much noise, for the Lord wasn't deaf, and he knows our hearts. Do you know what I said to these dull professors who were ashamed to speak about their faith? I said, 'You know the devil isn't deaf either, but that don't stop his followers making a great noise. I've got more to shout about than they! The devil would rather see us doubting than shouting!'[20]

He had his critics within the Church as well as outside it. In reply, he quoted Charles Wesley's hymn:

> My God, I am thine; What a comfort divine,
> What a blessing to know that my Jesus is mine!
> In the heavenly Lamb
> Thrice happy I am,
> And my heart it doth dance at the sound of his name.[21]

That same hymn was a favourite of my Wesleyan grandfather, who would quote it in his sermons. In one of these, he cited 'My heart it doth dance at the sound of his name', and added ruefully, 'There's not much religion in dancing at the moment; and not much dancing in religion – more's the pity!' Billy Bray would have concurred, or rather shouted a loud 'Amen'. In justifying what many folk regarded as his 'antics', he went behind the Wesley hymns to their source in Scripture. He identified keenly with the Psalmist, when he confessed: 'Thou hast turned for me my mourning into dancing: thou hast put off my sackcloth, and girded me with gladness: to the end that my glory may sing praise to thee, and not be silent. O Lord my God, I will give thanks to thee for ever' (Psalm 30:11–12 AV). He recalled King David, who 'danced before the Lord with all his might', when the Ark of the Covenant was brought back in procession. Nor was David deterred by the scorn of his wife, Michal, who 'looked through a window, and saw King David leaping and dancing before the Lord; and she despised him in her heart' (2 Samuel 6:14, 16 AV) Billy Bray used the incident in his own defence. He asked his critics: 'If David had something to dance about and leap about because he was bringing back the ark of the Lord to where it did belong ... don't we have much more to dance and shout about than he did? Why we've got the Lord himself!'[22]

From Cornish Methodism to the Orthodoxy of Holy Russia may seem a quantum leap. Yet is it fanciful to see some marks of family likeness between Billy Bray and the great St Seraphim of Sarov (1759–1833), whose life, hard and ascetic as it was, overflowed with joy? Seraphim, born into a merchant family, became a monk in the religious community of Sarov, and then, for nearly thirty years, lived as a hermit in the great forest that bordered the monastery. For the last eight years of his life he came out of seclusion, and opened the door of his cell to any who wished to seek him out. Innumerable visitors, enquirers and penitents beat a path to his door, as they did to that of his contemporary in France, St John Vianney, the Curé d'Ars (1786–1859). In Christian tradition and spirituality there is a clear sense in which Seraphim was light-years away from Billy Bray, the Cornish Methodist tin-miner. Yet in the dispensation of the Spirit, they were surely kinsmen. Iulia de Beausobre, in her vivid sketch of Seraphim, *Flame in the Snow,* shows us a man whose life was transfigured by joy:

> Seraphim's joy – the joy of the creature that constantly gazes at its creator – was so full that he sometimes thought it must tear down the walls of his cell. They stood stolidly. And so he left them from time to time in the dead of night, and ventured beyond the Sarov walls to roam among hushed trees, under twinkling stars. But most of his nights he still spent in prayer, and his days were devoted to any one who chose to come.[23]

On one occasion, a young monk and novice, filled with autumn melancholy and sadness at the sorrows of the world, unexpectedly encountered Seraphim. His garb was outlandish – 'his white habit, pulled up in front and behind, bulged funnily at the waist: he had stuffed it into his belt as he did when at work. At the sides, it hung low. A very large, bright green shawl, flung about him, fluttered in the wind. One end was caught round his neck and tied there; another trailed on the ground behind.' He no doubt looked a freak; but his joy, expressed in a kind of song and dance, Billy Bray would have understood:

> His eyes flashed, his step was almost that of a dance. With outstretched arms he came close up to the young men and gave them his blessing. He sang, 'Fill my heart

with joy, St. Mary, conqueror of the sin of sorrow, vessel gladly bearing joy.' Then taking hold of their hands he called out, 'Away with despondency. There is nothing Christ has not conquered. Nothing.'

At his approach, their mood had calmed, and mirrored his. Their anguish was gone, and they smiled. Singing, he continued on his way, his thin white hair blowing in the cold wind.[24]

Iulia de Beausobre calls her biographical essay on St Seraphim, *Flame in the Snow.* Whether in the snows of Russia, or in the mines of Cornwall, these men knew their hearts strangely warmed. It would be foolish to deny or minimize the great differences between Orthodoxy and Methodism; but there are also profound resonances, as I have tried to show. If we drill down to bedrock, we can find common ground.

6

METHODISM AND CATHOLICISM

ON 1ST JUNE 1978, the Methodist scholar, Dr Marcus Ward, was marking an end-of-term batch of examination scripts, when he suddenly and quietly collapsed and died at his desk. It was a fitting end to a most active and fruitful ministry. Like John Wesley, Marcus would have hated to be inactive, and would surely have endorsed Wesley's own prayer that he might 'cease at once to work and live'.

Marcus Ward had retired in 1972 from his post as New Testament tutor at Richmond College, where Methodist ordinands were trained. Even in retirement, however, he continued to do some teaching. For the last six years of his life he taught not Methodists, but Roman Catholics. To his surprise and delight, he was invited to join the staff of Heythrop College (University of London), a seminary run by the Jesuits, in Cavendish Square.

Heythrop, caught up in the reforms and renewal inspired by the Second Vatican Council (1962–65), had uprooted itself from the Oxfordshire countryside and settled in the heart of London's West End. The college took seriously the call of the Council to active ecumenical endeavour, and so invited Marcus Ward to teach New Testament for two days a week to its ordinands. He had his own room in the college, and was completely at home with his students and colleagues. His old friend and fellow-tutor from Richmond days, Norman Goldhawk, recalled the satisfaction which this new appointment gave to Marcus, as a veteran ecumenist:

I believe he looked upon his last years at Heythrop as

in many ways the fitting climax of his life-work. He told me with much satisfaction of how he would preach at a college Mass and remain in the special place they provided for him during the Communion – separated to a degree and yet basically one with them.

To those who knew Marcus Ward at this period, his sense of joy and fulfilment was patent. He was still in his first term at Heythrop when he happened to overhear a telephone conversation, of which he was the subject, and which delighted him. The caller asked a Jesuit member of staff, at whose elbow Marcus was standing, 'You've got Marcus Ward, the Methodist, with you now, haven't you? How's he getting on?' Marcus purred on hearing the reply: 'Oh, he's getting on splendidly; I think you could say of Marcus that he has the "*anima naturaliter Jesuitica*" (the naturally Jesuit mind).'

Why was Marcus Ward so utterly at home at Heythrop? It was, after all, a rare thing in England in the 1970s for a Methodist minister to be authorized to help train Roman Catholic priests. Admittedly, Marcus already knew many of his Jesuit colleagues from contacts in the University of London, and that no doubt oiled the wheels. He had already spent a lifetime in ecumenical work. Moreover, he was a most friendly and sociable man, with a strong sense of pastoral care for his students, and a born teacher. Yet there is more to be said, I believe, over and above the personal equation. At a deeper level, he was at home in the life and worship of Heythrop because his native Methodist spirituality predisposed him to it. Methodism is historically a variant of Evangelical Protestantism; but it has also a Catholic dimension to it, which goes back to the Wesleys, and which Marcus Ward strikingly exemplified.

I mentioned in chapter 1 the Methodist Sacramental Fellowship (MSF) as one manifestation of the Catholic element in Methodism. Marcus Ward was one of its founder-members. The Fellowship came to birth in the 1930s, among a group of Methodist ministers and laity who shared three basic concerns. They sought a more ordered and disciplined life of devotion. They wanted to maintain and develop the

Catholic emphases of the Wesleys, particularly the rich sacramental devotion of their eucharistic hymns. They were committed to the corporate reunion of all Christian people.

As it happened, reunion was very much to the fore on the
domestic Methodist scene of the 1930s. The year 1932 saw
the union of three former branches of Methodism: the Wesleyans, the Primitives, and the United Methodists (this last
itself a union of several smaller groups). Together they
formed the present Methodist Church of Great Britain, but
they represented quite different strands of piety and church
order. The Primitive and United Methodists had virile traditions of preaching, evangelism and lay participation; but
in the nature of the case, being largely non-Wesleyan in
origin, they lacked the strong sacramental devotion of the
Wesleys. They saw themselves as much closer to the older
English Free Churches than to the Anglican Church from
which the Wesleyans traced their origins. The Wesleyans who
founded the MSF feared that the Catholic strand in their
tradition might be diluted or submerged within the newly
united Church. Moreover, they were alarmed at secularizing
tendencies, even within Wesleyan Methodism itself. As Dr
J. E. Rattenbury, an outstanding leader of the MSF, testified,
the younger ministers who formed the Fellowship saw it
as 'the only way to arrest certain secularizing tendencies in
the Church', by standing together 'in the united loyalty
of a devotional fellowship for the fundamental truths of
Christianity and primarily for the personal practice of the
devout life.'

Like Newman and his colleagues of the Oxford Movement
in the 1830s, these Methodists became suspect in their own
church as 'Romanizers'. To be fair, opponents of the MSF
could legitimately point to the fact that in 1935, the year in
which the Fellowship was formed, one of its leading architects, T. S. Gregory, left the Methodist ministry for the
Church of Rome. Gregory, an outstanding preacher and
spiritual guide, published the story of his conversion in *The
Unfinished Universe* (1935). Its Preface begins:

I wrote this book as a Methodist minister, and began

work upon it without any suspicion that I should ever
become anything else. There are questions – so it
seemed to me – which must assail any sincere Christian
in these days, some of faith and others of practice; and
it was in attempting to find a Christian answer to them
that I was led into the Catholic faith.

These questions of Christian faith and practice he had
begun to agonize over prior to 1935, along with some of the
men who originated the MSF. Some of them followed 'T.S.',
as Gregory was universally known to his friends, into the
Catholic Church. One such was the Reverend Bill Barr, who
was to give distinguished service to the Society of St Vincent
de Paul. On its own modest scale, T.S.'s leaving Methodism
for Rome caused almost as much ferment and heart-search-
ing as Newman's departure from the Church of England for
the same destination.

Gregory was not just another Methodist minister. He was
one of the rising hopes of the Wesleyan ministry and of
the newly united Church of 1932. He came from a classic
Methodist family. His father and his cousin (A. S. Gregory,
also a member of the MSF) were both ministers. After reading Greats at Oxford, he taught at Handsworth College,
Birmingham, and from there went on to an influential pastoral and preaching ministry. He once told me that, when
he was a minister in York, his preaching became so caught
up with the questions of faith that were agitating him and
drawing him – unwittingly at this stage – to Rome, that
he thought he must have been largely unintelligible to his
congregation. 'I think', he added, 'that perhaps the only
one of them who had any idea what I was driving at was one
perceptive teenager, who was to become a lifelong friend –
Christopher Hill, later Master of Balliol.'

The year 1935, then, the year of the MSF's birth, of T. S.
Gregory's departure for Rome, and the publication of his
Apologia, really set the cat among the pigeons in official
Methodism. Understandably, ex-Primitive and ex-United
Methodists were especially alarmed at what they saw as a
threat to the union they had so recently entered. Their fears

71

were shared by some ex-Wesleyans. Many leading Methodists suspected the MSF of being a subversive body, undermining Protestant faith and practice, and seducing younger ministers to Rome. It was no surprise, therefore, when in 1937 the Methodist Conference set up a committee of enquiry to examine the MSF. The committee reported to the 1938 annual Conference, which met in Hull.

The venue had more than geographical significance. Hull, like the Potteries and County Durham, was one of the strongholds of the former Primitive Methodist Church. The 'Prims', as they were colloquially known, had some understandable misgivings about the Methodist Union of 1932. They feared a Wesleyan take-over, being outnumbered by the larger and older body. They treasured a form of worship less formal, more charismatic in style, than that of the sober Wesleyans. Their church order gave a much stronger role to the laity than the more clericalized Wesleyan polity. Moreover, Ernest Rattenbury, the High Wesleyan President of the MSF from 1938 to 1950, was already well known as one of the leading opponents of the union scheme of 1932. He argued that it conceded too much of the Wesleyan heritage of ministry and order, for the sake of reaching consensus. He feared that the Methodist realignment would put at risk a future union with the Church of England. In the event, he accepted the Wesleyan Conference decision to unite with Primitive and United Methodists, but his stubborn rearguard action left him a marked man in the eyes of his opponents. It was with this personal record that he stood up at Hull to defend the MSF – a High churchman in a Low church stronghold.

His speech was masterly. He found the Report only 'mildly condemnatory of the Fellowship', and welcomed the fact that, 'not a sign is to be found in it of the violent criticisms of twelve months ago'. The speech was later published as an MSF pamphlet, *In Defence of the Methodist Sacramental Fellowship*. It reads as a closely reasoned rebuttal of the Report's charge that the MSF was 'out of harmony with Methodist teaching and practice'. The printed speech was prefaced by the stated aims of the Fellowship, which Rattenbury proceeded to expound and defend. They were:

(1) Re-affirmation of the FAITH that inspired the Evangelical Revival and the hymns of the Wesleys – the Faith that is formulated in the Nicene Creed.
(2) Making THE HOLY COMMUNION central in the life of the Methodist Church.
(3) RE-UNION. Adhering to the principles of the Reformation, yet being convinced that the divisions of the Church Militant are becoming ever more clearly contrary to the will of GOD, the Fellowship works and prays for the corporate re-union of all believers.[1]

Rattenbury had no difficulty in defending the modest requirement that MSF members should receive Communion at least monthly. Far from being an extreme demand, he argued, it fell well short of Wesley's own ideal and practice:

Wesley communicated all through his ministry approximately twice a week. He celebrated or received Holy Communion every Sunday morning. When he formed the Bands [i.e. early, small fellowship groups], one of his rules was that every member of them should receive the Sacrament once a week. When towards the close of his life he formed the American Methodist Church he advised the ministers to celebrate Holy Communion every Sunday.

It seems clear that by the 1930s Wesleyan Methodists had fallen away from the practice of their pious founder. Having cited Wesley, Dr Rattenbury adds, 'I am not claiming that this should necessarily be our modern Methodist Standard, but I do say that it is preposterous to quote Wesley against those who only impose on their members a reception of Holy Communion once a month as if they were Sacramentalists in a sense in which he was not.'[2] In a longer look at the Methodist theological tradition, he denies that the MSF is in any sense 'out of harmony' with it: 'Our views are those of John and Charles Wesley; Adam Clarke; W. B. Pope, our greatest theologian; Hugh Price Hughes our greatest

Evangelist; and John Scott Lidgett the greatest of living Free Churchmen.'[3]

The Conference Report acknowledged the right of the MSF to exist within Methodism, but concluded: 'In our judgement "the Sacramental Fellowship" has isolated the Lord's Supper from other means of grace, and has given the Sacrament a position which is not in harmony with the teaching and practice of the Methodist Church.' Against that claim Rattenbury argued that, in so far as it was true, it was because Methodism itself had fallen away from the sacramental faith and practice of the Wesleys.

There was, of course, a hidden agenda, which Rattenbury insisted on bringing out into the open: 'When the Methodist people criticised the MSF', he urged, 'they were really thinking of matters not mentioned in the Report at all, the alleged ritual practices and Romanizing tendencies of the Fellowship.' He rebutted these charges, and gave amusing examples of what passed for 'popery' with some of the Methodist people. 'Only a short time since a minister told me that he asked a village congregation to read with him alternate verses from one of the psalms appended to the new hymn book, and the next day received a letter from two members stating they would resign if ever these popish practices were repeated!' Rattenbury urged Conference not to 'encourage those who by the stale cry of "No Popery" hamper every attempt to enrich worship and deepen reverence in the house of God.'[4]

Half a century later, the cry of 'No Popery' is still to be heard occasionally in Methodism; but it is vastly more rare, and infinitely staler than it was in 1938. For that, Dr Rattenbury must take some credit. Other influences, of course, have helped. The Liturgical Movement has had widespread and beneficial effects in Methodism, as in all the Churches, and has brought considerable enrichment of worship. In 1938, as Rattenbury testified, for a minister to wear a preaching gown was often to arouse anti-ritualistic fervour. Today, cassock, gown and bands are normal liturgical dress for many Methodist ministers, while a younger generation increasingly favours the wearing of a cassock-alb.

74

That, in Rattenbury's day, would infallibly have shrieked of Rome.

Rattenbury, then, convinced the Conference that the MSF had a right to life, though the Romanizing smear was to cling to the Fellowship for a long time. The crucial question, however, remained: was the Fellowship simply a High Church party to be grudgingly tolerated; or did it represent a vital and authentic part of the Wesleyan tradition? To answer that question, we must call in evidence the eucharistic hymns of John and Charles Wesley, first published in 1745. Significantly, one of the earliest publications of the MSF was a *Selection of Hymns on the Lord's Supper*,[5] chosen from the Wesleys, which appeared in 1936. There is a rich vein of sacramental devotion in these hymns, which the MSF wanted to make freely available, to Methodists and other Christians. In the half-century since they were published, Anglicans and Roman Catholics have also begun to discover them, to their own acknowledged benefit.[6]

The Wesleys' *Hymns on the Lord's Supper* numbered 166 in all, of which the MSF reproduced fifty-three. Dr Rattenbury, in his *The Eucharistic Hymns of John and Charles Wesley* (1948) reprinted the whole collection, and dedicated his study to 'The members of the Methodist Sacramental Fellowship'. This highlighting of the eucharistic hymns by the MSF contrasts rather markedly with their treatment in twentieth-century Methodist hymnbooks. The 1933 *Methodist Hymn Book*, issued for the newly united Church just prior to the foundation of the MSF, contains only a dozen or so of the hymns. True, some of the finest are included, like 'Victim divine, thy grace we claim', with its triumphant affirmation of the Real Presence:

> We need not now go up to heaven,
>   To bring the long-sought Saviour down;
> Thou art to all already given,
>   Thou dost even now Thy banquet crown.
> To every faithful soul appear,
> And show Thy real presence here.[7]

Yet some of the choicest are not included in the eucharistic section of the book, but placed elsewhere, as if their sacramental theology were too strong meat for the stomach of the compilers. Thus Wesley's 'O God of our forefathers, hear' is found, not under 'Hymns for the Lord's Supper', but under the generalized heading of 'The Church in Prayer'. Yet the eucharistic intention of the hymn is transparent:

> With solemn faith we offer up,
> And spread before Thy glorious eyes,
> That only ground of all our hope,
> That precious, bleeding sacrifice,
> Which brings Thy grace on sinners down,
> And perfects all our souls in one.[8]

Wesley is not speaking of a repetition or re-enactment of the once-for-all sacrifice of Calvary. Rather, in the Eucharist the Church pleads that one, all-prevailing offering, and claims in the sacrament all the benefits of Christ's Passion.

Hymns and Psalms, the Methodist hymn book published in 1983, kept most of the dozen or so eucharistic hymns from the 1933 book, and took the opportunity to add one or two more. One welcome addition was 'See where our great High Priest/Before the Lord appears', with its splendid second verse on the solidarity of the Church with Christ:

> With him the corner-stone
> The living stones conjoin;
> Christ and his church are one,
> One body and one vine;
> For us he uses all his powers
> And all he has, or is, is ours.[9]

The compilers also included Charles Wesley's hymn on the disciples' encounter with the Risen Lord on the road to Emmaus, with Gordon Slater's superbly matching tune, 'St Botolph':

> O Thou who this mysterious bread
>   Didst in Emmaus break,
> Return, herewith, our souls to feed,
>   And to thy followers speak.[10]

Hymns and Psalms also included two of the Wesley sacramental hymns on the Epiclesis. The first calls upon the Spirit to energize the sacramental elements:

> Come, Holy Ghost, thine influence shed,
>   And realize the sign;
> Thy life infuse into the bread,
>   Thy power into the wine.[11]

The second hymn invokes the Holy Spirit to descend upon the worshipping people:

> Come, thou witness of his dying;
>   Come, remembrancer divine,
> Let us feel thy power, applying
>   Christ to every soul, and mine.[12]

This Catholic tradition in the life of Methodism was to a large extent overlaid in the nineteenth century. The Oxford Movement and the Catholic Revival in the Church of England tended, by reaction, to drive Wesleyan Methodists to make common cause with the historic English Free Churches. Yet the Catholic tradition never died out among the Wesleyans, and even before it flowered afresh in the Methodist Sacramental Fellowship, it found some notable exponents. Hugh Price Hughes, the fiery Celt who founded the West London Mission, was both ardent preacher and committed sacramentalist. Sir Henry Lunn (1859–1939) was in the same tradition. His was a colourful and many-sided career, both within and outside Methodism. He was an ordained Wesleyan minister, a surgeon, and a medical missionary in India. Invalided home after a breakdown in health, he quarrelled with the Wesleyan authorities over missionary policy. He believed vehemently that European missionaries should identify with the life of the local people, rather than enjoying a standard of living which made them a class apart. He was a passionate ecumenist and, as a spin-off from the Grindelwald conferences on church unity which he organized in Switzerland, founded the Lunn Travel Agency, which proved a notable commercial success. He shared the MSF's aims of a disciplined devotional life, a strong sacramental emphasis, and a commitment to Christian reunion. While remaining a Methodist, he was also confirmed in the Anglican Church, and the *Dictionary of National Biography* describes his religious position as 'that of Wesley, a Methodist member of the Anglican Church'.[13]

Sir Henry was also an influential author. Though his books ante-date the formation of the MSF, they anticipate its concern for the deepening of the life of Christian devotion. In books like *The Love of Jesus* (1911), *Retreats for the Soul* (1918), and *The Secret of the Saints* (1933), he drew widely on the classics of Christian prayer and meditation. He was happy to reprint Puritans like Richard Baxter, or Quakers like George Fox and John Greenleaf Whittier. Predictably, he drew copiously on the hymns of the Wesleys. Yet he made extensive raids into Anglican and Catholic territory, and came back with his hands full of rich spoils. Augustine, Bernard, Francis, à Kempis, the Ignatian Exercises, Teresa of Avila; George Herbert, Lancelot Andrewes, Jeremy Taylor, Thomas Wilson: these were the authors he laid under frequent contribution and sought to share with a Protestant readership. In the ecumenical journal he founded, *The Review of the Churches*, he strove to advance the cause of corporate Christian unity. In his devotional writings he sought to bring together the riches of Christian devotion in the Free Church, Anglican and Roman Catholic traditions.

The sceptic can point to the fact that Henry's son, Arnold, became a Roman Catholic layman, and his grandson, David, a Benedictine monk; as if that nullified his efforts for unity. It did not. Whatever may have been the later decisions of his descendants, Henry Lunn remained firm in his position as an Anglican Methodist. His books deepened the faith and kindled the devotion of thousands who had not the slightest intention of converting to Rome. William Newton, my own Wesleyan grandfather, was a staunch Protestant and Evangelical; but he treasured his copy of Henry Lunn's *The Secret of the Saints.*

The same tradition was maintained in the ministry of A. E. Whitham (1879–1938), the first President of the MSF. In reporting his death, the *Methodist Recorder* spoke of his 'deep understanding of the teaching of the saints, and his great catholicity of outlook [which] infused his preaching and lecturing with a unique atmosphere and charm, and greatly enhanced the evangelical appeal of his ministry.' The titles of his books bear out that judgement, and clearly reflect the priorities of the Methodist Sacramental Fellowship: *The Discipline and Culture of the Spiritual Life* (1938); *The Pastures of His Presence* (1939); and *The Catholic Christ* (1940). He was an intensely loyal Methodist, yet with a great breadth of Christian sympathy. Harold Darby, a close friend, testified to his catholicity: he was 'ardent in zeal for the catholic treasures of all Christendom, but ready to lead a women's meeting with a Sankey hymn'.

A. E. Whitham's *The Catholic Christ* reveals the roots of his sacramental theology. He will have no truck with a falsely spiritualized, ethereal religion, which does not take created things with the reverence warranted by the Incarnation. Typical of his writing is his essay on Lenten observance, entitled 'Acts of Discipline'. His thesis is that we need to discipline, not deny, our senses, and he urges:

> Perhaps the surest way of throwing off the unhallowed power of the senses would be by a frank use of the senses in our religious life . . . We might . . . use flowers and pictures and other simple furniture of devotion in our prayer-room, accustom ourselves to prayers of thanksgiving for all delights of nature, for all colour in life, for the presence of friends, the shining eye, the responsive smile, the tender voice, the warm physical presence of those we love or count as friends.[14]

Again, in a peculiarly pregnant passage of an essay on 'The

Soul and the Senses', Whitham writes of the key importance for Christianity of 'time and space, flesh and body':

> When the supreme revelation of history is made, it is the fulness of the Godhead *bodily*. When that same revelation is handed down through the ages, it is by means of the Church which is His *Body*. When that revelation becomes most intimately mine, it is through a meal – 'Take, eat; this is My *body*.'

He drives the same lesson home from aesthetic experience:

> The body is not the soul. But here in this terrestrial life we know nothing of soul save through the body. Every spiritual good comes to us through the senses. Music that intoxicates my soul first strikes the drum of the ear in physical vibration. Painting – though of a Madonna or of our Blessed Lord, compelling me to pray – must come as thoroughfare by the pedestrian way of the senses to my spirit. Literature – the music of the soul – is first a matter of sight or sound; yes, and thought itself. William of Occam long ago observed, 'There is nothing in the mind that was not first in the senses.'

All this bears directly on Whitham's strong sacramental theology. He begins with the sacrament of the gospel, which conveys to us all that God has done for us in Christ, and working outwards from that centre-point, he finds the whole universe sacramental:

> Many who talk loudly of finding God everywhere don't really mean what they say, especially when they are thinking of the sacrament. They really mean they find God alongside the bread, the bread which is a suspicious, dangerous accompaniment. But when I say I find God, I mean in the bread as I found him in the Incarnate Jesus, and as I found Him in the Church. For the Church is the extension of the Incarnation, and implies the same frank acceptance of the world of sense as a tabernacle of God; and the Sacrament is an extension of the Incarnation and the Cross, and therefore the

most glorious, the most wondrous, the most gracious function of the Church.

The movement is from the particular to the general, from the special God-given time and place, outwards to all times and places:

> Christianity is concerned with the particular and con-crete – begins at a particular place in a particular time; and from those precious embodiments I pass on to universal thoughts. Here in this mother and child, then in all birth and childhood; in the face of this man, then in the face of every brother; in this man's pain on Calvary, then in all pain; in the darkness of His Gethsemane, then to be found as treasure in all dark-ness; in this meal then in every meal; until the whole visible world is aglow with the light of God.[15]

These truths were lucidly expounded by T. S. Gregory when, after half a lifetime as a Roman Catholic, he found himself at home again in a Methodist gathering. It was 1966, and the Second Vatican Council had sounded its trumpet-call to Roman Catholics to engage in active ecumenism. The Methodist School of Fellowship, in which Gregory had once played a leading role, was meeting at Swanwick, Derbyshire, for its annual conference. T. S. was invited to be 'chaplain' to the School, to lead the prayers and give a series of devotional addresses. Some of the members found it odd that a Roman Catholic should be given this role. Yet although he had been a Catholic for thirty years, in his spirituality T. S. had never ceased to be a Methodist. He accepted the invitation, pro-vided that the Catholic Bishop of Nottingham, in whose diocese Swanwick lay, would give consent. He did so, and Gregory led the Methodists into the rich heritage of their own Wesleyan spirituality.

He gave four addresses, later published as *According to your Faith*, which are a moving exposition of the Wesley hymns. He expounds the hymns as one who has lived and prayed them for a lifetime. In interpreting the Church as the Body of Christ, Gregory emphasizes that:

81

This Body is a real body, a living organism, and I am a member of it. The Word was made flesh, and that flesh is ours, the body and blood of Jesus Christ the Son of God. Our union with Him does not rest ultimately upon what we think or believe or will but upon the Incarnation, 'that which we have seen with our eyes and our hands handled', and upon the act that made Him bodily Man.

> My Jesus to know,
> And feel his blood flow,
> 'Tis life everlasting, 'tis heaven below.

It is an intimacy and organic union *below*.

Charles Wesley never inherited, never entertained the dualism which severs mind from body. At the lowest reckoning he knew that many kinds of human sin are of the flesh; but he also believed in the resurrection of the body. Into this earthly being God breathed the life He made eternal. It is this corruptible that must put on incorruption.[16]

Gregory then goes on, quite naturally, to quote Wesley's eucharistic hymns:

> O let us on thy fulness feed
> And eat thy flesh and drink thy blood;
> Jesu, thy blood is drink indeed;
> Jesu, thy flesh is angels' food.

He then cites John 6:51, part of the great discourse on Jesus as the Bread of Life: 'I am the living bread which came down out of heaven: if any man eat of this bread, he shall live for ever: yea and the bread which I shall give is my flesh, for the life of the world.' That reference leads Gregory to another of the *Hymns on the Lord's Supper*:

> This eucharistic feast
> Our every want supplies;

And still we by his death are blessed,
  And share his sacrifice.

We too are with him dead,
  And shall with him arise;
The cross on which he bows his head
  Shall lift us to the skies.

So Gregory is led to the conclusion of his third address, in which he has set forth the meaning of the Incarnation through the medium of Charles Wesley's hymns:

> This was the essence of Charles Wesley's gospel, for it means at least that there is no human carnality that the divine Incarnation does not reach and sanctify, no fleshy thing in our mortal experience below lies outside the divine-human organism or eludes the 'bleeding prince of life and peace'. So the squalor is not rejected but washed and made holy, the commonplaces have their home in Nazareth, Golgotha meets Paradise, and man's physical being with all its needs and pains and servitude enters the Kingdom of Heaven.[17]

The created order, matter, the body, are not, then, written off, or written down, for the sake of some bloodless cult of spirituality. They are affirmed as holy, God-given, meant to be the media and channels of his grace. In short, they are sacramental. Hence the importance of the bread and wine of the Eucharist, made by God's grace the bearers of Christ's divine humanity. In Charles Wesley's words, they are 'effectual tokens' – 'Fit channels to convey Thy love/to every faithful heart'.

Ernest Rattenbury, Henry Lunn, A. E. Whitham and T. S. Gregory were distinguished representatives of the Catholic Methodist tradition in the earlier part of the twentieth century. But what of the tradition today? Has it held up and been maintained? Or has it been largely sidelined and overtaken by events? We might apply to this strand of Methodism the question members of the annual Methodist Conference quaintly put to themselves in the words of the traditional opening hymn, 'And are we yet alive/And see each other's face?' The writings of Neville Ward (cousin of Dr Marcus Ward) and Gordon Wakefield provide ample evidence of that. These are not peripheral authors, but among the most widely read in Methodism. They also speak, of course, to many Christians outside the Methodist tradition. Younger scholars include David Butler, Neil Dixon, Norman Wallwork and Michael Townsend, whose published work combines Methodism and Catholicity.

Again, we might point to the ministry of Dr Donald Soper – Baron Soper of Kingsway – who is arguably the best-known Methodist of his generation. Donald Soper is not merely the successor of Hugh Price Hughes and Ernest Rattenbury, as the Superintendent of the West London Mission. He is also heir to their strong Wesleyan sacramental tradition. Outstanding preacher, orator, open-air controversialist that he is, his life and ministry have been rooted in the Eucharist. For many years he has been President of the Methodist Sacramental Fellowship, like Rattenbury before him. His preaching ministry has been distinguished, but for him Christianity has never been simply a religion of the Word. It has always been the faith of the Word Incarnate, the Word made flesh. It therefore takes material things, the creatures, with intense seriousness. It never disparages materiality, nor degrades it in the name of the 'spiritual'. As C. S. Lewis neatly expresses it, 'God likes matter; he invented it.'

I hope I have said enough to show what a rich vein of truly Catholic theology and devotion there is in Methodism, not least through the witness of the Methodist Sacramental Fellowship and the writings of its members. The Catholic strand in Methodism is by no means the predominant one, nor the only one; but Methodism would be infinitely poorer without it.

7

GRASPING THE NETTLE:
THE ECUMENICAL SOCIETY OF THE
BLESSED VIRGIN MARY

THE ECUMENICAL QUEST is not for faint-hearted pilgrims, who give up easily when the going gets rough. Those who are seriously committed to the unity of separated Christians must face what Sir John Lawrence pinpointed as 'the hard facts of unity'. Inevitably, it is a long haul. The divisions of centuries are not going to be healed by applying the sticking plaster of some quick doctrinal fix. There are stubborn stereotypes to be broken down, and grotesque caricatures to be corrected. Charity is essential, but it is not enough. Even if the milk of human kindness were to flow like a river, it could not of itself wash away all doctrinal barriers and purge the silt of centuries.

Any ecumenist of integrity has to face strong differences of conviction, and profound issues of truth. In the Lord's high-priestly prayer of John 17, he prays, 'For their sake I consecrate myself, that they too may be consecrated by the truth . . . may they all be one: as thou, Father, art in me, and I in thee, so also may they be in us, that the world may believe that thou didst send me' (John 17:19, 21 NEB).

It was such a dogged commitment to unity in truth that drove Martin Gillet, the founder of the Ecumenical Society of the Blessed Virgin Mary, to set up a body which seemed certain to become a sign of contradiction. I first met Martin in 1978, soon after I had moved from Bristol to London, to take up the work of Superintendent of the West London Mission. He came to see me with a twofold aim. First, he wanted to tell me of the work of the Ecumenical Society, though that object was something of a sprat to catch a mackerel. His second objective was to persuade me to take the place on the Society's Council left vacant by the recent death of Marcus Ward.

I promised him I would think seriously about it, though I felt more than a little out of my depth in the area of Marian doctrine. On the other side, however, my long debt of friendship to Marcus Ward predisposed me to want to continue an aspect of his ecumenical work. Marcus was an ecumenist *extraordinaire*, as I tried to show in a biographical sketch, 'A Man for All Churches' (1984). Against that instinct to accept Martin's invitation to serve, I had to set my ignorance of the field, which was so great as almost to be distinguished. My Protestant, Methodist, Evangelical upbringing had never been tainted with vulgar anti-Romanism. I had never been indoctrinated with anti-Marian prejudice. At the same time, there was in our tradition a distinct reserve about the Virgin Mary. In our Christian scheme of things, she was not so much downgraded as ignored. At Wesley House, Cambridge, our theological tutor, Philip Watson, was a fine theologian and an expert Lutheran scholar. Yet in his dealing with Christology, he made scant reference to Mary, the Mother of the Lord. If a student happened to raise a question in this area, Philip would simply recommend the scholarly, but polemical work of Giovanni Miegge, *The Virgin Mary: The Roman Catholic Marian Doctrine* (1955). The blurb of this work spoke of 'the astonishing advancement of the Virgin Mary into membership of the Godhead', and Miegge's concluding sentence expressed a sombre fear of where Mariolatry was tending within the Roman Church. Writing before the Second Vatican Council, Miegge claimed that eventually Mary would completely usurp the place of Christ in the scheme of salvation, and asserted, 'On that day it will be said that within Catholicism Christianity has given up the field to a different religion' (p. 191).

When Neville Ward took his fellow-Methodists by surprise and wrote a book on the Rosary – *Five for Sorrow, Ten for Joy* (1971) – he gave two reasons for doing so. First, to use a method of prayer from another Christian tradition could give fresh stimulus to a pattern of devotion which could easily grow stale by routine. Secondly, he was concerned that 'in Methodism the silence about the Mother of Jesus is positively deafening'.[1] Yet even so committed an ecumenist as Raymond George was not impressed by this plea. He merely countered that the New Testament itself maintained a similarly deafening silence on the same subject.

If Methodist scholars showed such typical coolness towards Mary, those whom the sixteenth century labelled 'the hotter sort of Protestants' went much further. They are still with us, of course, and the name of Mary is apt to make a good deal of Evangelical flesh creep. To such Christians, it seems axiomatic that to exalt Mary must mean, in the same measure, to diminish the Lord Jesus Christ in his sovereign right as Redeemer. These were the kinds of consideration that made me hesitate to comply with Martin Gillett's request when he came to see me in my study at Kingsway Hall. Martin, however, was the sort of advocate who would rarely take no for an answer. He was a living exposition of the parable of the importunate widow, who so badgered the judge until she got her desire. He paid me several more visits and followed his calls with telephone conversations. Yet he was not in the business of sheer pressurization. He invited my questions, criticisms, and the free expression of misgivings. In return he was more than ready to give a reason for the faith that was in him – namely, that Mary, far from being a stumbling-block to Christian unity, could be a means of reconciliation.

The Quakers would have described Martin as a man with a 'concern', a burning conviction that God had laid upon his heart and mind a special calling and a task, which he must fulfil. He had been raised an Anglican, and as a young man had converted to Catholicism. He had the zeal of the convert, but it was a very unconventional zeal. His concern was not to make non-Catholic Christians in his own – Roman – image. What he longed for was to bring separated Christians into a deeper and fuller unity than any of them had yet known in their unreconciled state. How was it to be done? One sovereign way – his way, as he believed – was to

87

strengthen their understanding of Mary's place in the Church, and to deepen their devotion to her as the Mother of the Lord.

It seems at first sight, no doubt, a very cack-handed way of trying to foster the unity of Christian people. Conventional wisdom tells examination candidates to tackle first the questions on their paper about which they are most knowledgeable and confident. Time enough, after that, to frame up to the really knotty ones. Not so with the Martin Gillett approach. He wanted to grasp the nettle, and confront, firmly and irenically, one of the most divisive doctrines in post-Reformation history: the place of Mary in the Christian scheme of salvation. He made clear to me, however, that the Ecumenical Society was not interested in Mariology run riot. It was committed to a study of Mary's role in the Christian dispensation, but always in subordination to her Son, the unique Saviour of the world. The literature of the Society sets out its purpose with careful clarity: 'The Society exists to advance the study at various levels of the place of the Blessed Virgin Mary in the Church, under Christ, and of related theological questions; and in the light of such study to promote ecumenical devotion.'

It can hardly be coincidental, I think, that the Society was founded in 1967, so soon after the conclusion of the Second Vatican Council. Pope John XXIII, in summoning the first General Council of the Roman Church since 1869–70, threw open the windows of the Church, and let in a good deal of fresh light and air. In *De Ecclesia*, the Dogmatic Constitution on the Church, the Council Fathers had important and irenical things to say about Mary. They were conscious, no doubt, of the sometimes extravagant Marian devotion which had characterized popular piety in some parts of the Roman Catholic world. Many Catholics themselves were unhappy with such extravagance, and were often acutely aware of the offence it could give to members of the non-Roman churches.

Robert Macafee Brown, an American Presbyterian theologian, was one of the numerous non-Catholic observers who were invited to attend the Council. Such invitations were themselves an indicator of a new spirit of Catholic openness and readiness for informed dialogue and criticism. Brown describes, in his racy and informative *Observer in Rome* (1964), something of the strenuous in-fighting that took place among the Council fathers over Marian doctrine. The conservatives desperately wanted the Council to formulate a special document devoted to Mary, which would maximize her role in the scheme of salvation. A majority of bishops were of another mind, and determined that Mary should find her due place within the document on the Church. She might be its most distinguished member, but she belonged within the Church, along with her fellow-believers. One Rome newspaper announced the doctrinal decision in its own breezy, but approving style: 'Council Fathers vote Mary into Church.'

Chapter 8 of the Dogmatic Constitution on the Church sought to re-affirm Mary's vital role in the whole Christian scheme of salvation. At the same time, it engaged in critical dialogue with Marian doctrine and devotion, and sought to meet the critics at three crucial points. First, it emphasized Mary's humanity and creatureliness, against those who would elevate her to the status of a semi-divine being. As 'the Mother of the Redeemer', she 'far surpasses all other creatures, both in heaven and on earth'. She is the 'excellent exemplar in faith and charity' for all Christians. She is the Second Eve, who counteracts rebellion against God's purpose for human life by her complete obedience to his will, so that, in the words of Irenaeus, 'What the virgin Eve bound through her unbelief, Mary loosened by her faith.' Yet for all that, Mary remains a creature, human, of the same nature as all other members of the Church: 'Because she belongs to the offspring of Adam she is one with all human beings in their need for salvation.'[2]

Secondly, Mary is placed firmly within the Church, not above it. Christ alone is the supreme Head of the Church. Mary, in accord with the Gospel promise ('All generations shall call me blessed', Luke 1:48) is entitled to special reverence as the Mother of the Lord. She is the Church's leading member; but she is a member still.

Thirdly, the Second Vatican Council deliberately closed the door against all baroque developments of Marian piety, which would see Mary as co-Redemptrix with her Son. The Fathers are as uncompromising as the most fervent Protestant here: 'We have but one Mediator, as we know from the words of the Apostle: "For there is one God, and one mediator between God and men, himself man, Christ Jesus, who gave himself a ransom for all" (1 Timothy 2:5–6). The maternal duty of Mary toward men in no way obscures or diminishes this unique mediation of Christ, but rather shows its power.'[3] Lest the point should not be taken, the Fathers underscore it. Mary's maternal love for Christians, and her continuing prayer for the Church, '. . . neither take away from nor add anything to the dignity and efficacy of Christ the one Mediator'.[4]

These careful attempts to prune back the more luxuriant growths of Marian devotion were no doubt music in the ears of some Protestants who read the documents. Others no doubt remained stubbornly unconvinced. It is true, the text takes for granted the dogmas of Mary's immaculate conception, perpetual virginity, and assumption into heaven. These doctrines even ecumenically-minded Protestants would tend to treat with very considerable reserve. At best, they might regard the dogmas as 'pious opinions' rather than as belonging to the substance of the faith.

Nevertheless, Protestants can well appreciate the warning given to Catholic theologians in this same document:

> . . . that in treating of the unique dignity of the Mother of God, they carefully and equally avoid the falsity of exaggeration on the one hand, and the excess of narrow-mindedness on the other . . . Let them painstakingly guard against any word or deed which could lead separated brethren or anyone else into error regarding the doctrine of the Church.[5]

The document ends on a note which Martin Gillet must have relished. Its closing paragraph acknowledges that 'it gives great joy and comfort to this most holy Synod that among the separated brethren, too, there are those who give due honour to the Mother of our Lord and Saviour.'[6]

That, certainly, has been my experience within the Ecumenical Society. Its membership goes well beyond the predictable Roman Catholics, High Anglicans and Orthodox. It numbers also within its ranks Baptists, Lutherans, Presbyterians, Congregationalists, United Reformed Church members, and Anglican Evangelicals. Nor are these latter unrepresentative mavericks. They are loyal, mainstream members of their own Churches, who have been drawn to the mystery of Mary, the Mother of the Lord.

One swallow does not make a summer; and yet these Protestant members of the Society may, I think, be a small, but significant indicator of change. Where Mary is concerned, they enable us to tap the ecumenical barometer, and find a new reading. The needle has assuredly not swung to 'outlook settled'; but at least it is not fixated at 'stormy'.

What evidence is there to show for such an alleged change, apart from the membership of the Ecumenical Society itself? Is it all a piece of ecumenical self-deception and wishful thinking? I judge not. As a Methodist, I would want to call in evidence here the content of *Hymns and Psalms*, which is sub-titled 'A Methodist and Ecumenical Hymn Book'. It was prepared, we are told, 'by representatives of the British Methodist Conference and by members of the Baptist Union, Churches of Christ, Church of England, Congregational Federation, Methodist Church in Ireland, United Reformed Church, and the Wesleyan Reform Union'.

The compilers of the hymn book, according to their Preface, 'have sought to recognize the many changes that have taken place, both inside and outside the Christian Church, since the publication of the great 1933 book'. They aimed to combine the best of ancient and modern hymnody, and so to include 'the riches of classical, evangelical, catholic, and charismatic hymnody of the past and the present'.

The doctrinal content of the new hymn book is significant for Methodists, who have traditionally sung their faith, as well as confessing it in the classic creeds of the Church.

Interestingly, then, the new book includes, for the first time, a number of hymns devoted to Mary, the Mother of the Lord. There is, for example, the Basque Carol of the Annunciation, which begins:

> The Angel Gabriel from heaven came,
> His wings as drifted snow, his eyes as flame;
> 'All hail', said he, 'thou lowly maiden Mary,
> Most highly favoured lady,'
> Gloria![7]

There is also a hymn of the Presentation of the Christ child:

> Hail to the Lord who comes,
>   Comes to his temple gate!
> Not with his angel host,
> Not in his kingly state . . .
>
> But borne upon the throne
>   Of Mary's gentle breast,
> Watched by her duteous love,
>   In her fond arms at rest;
> Thus to his Father's house
> He comes, the heavenly Guest.[8]

Within the section of hymns on the Eucharist, we have Patrick Appleford's,

> Lord Jesus Christ,
> You have come to us,
> You are one with us,
>   Mary's Son . . .

All these hymns have to do with the Incarnation of the Lord, the Word made flesh. They bring into focus the truth that whoever says 'Jesus', must also say 'Mary', because he is always and for ever, 'Mary's Son'. She it was who bore him, suckled him at her breast, shaped him, loved him with the unique love of a mother. Kipling's lines are no doubt hackneyed, but they express a profound truth:

> If I were hanged on the highest hill,
> Mother o' mine, O mother o' mine!
> I know whose love would follow me still,
> Mother o' mine, O mother o' mine!

New Testament scholars debate whether Mary did in fact stand at the foot of the cross where her Son died; but in her heart she could be nowhere else.

For my part, I have come increasingly to see that Mary is utterly central to a religion of the Word made flesh. Jesus is born of the Spirit of God; but he is also bone of her bone, and flesh of her flesh. She opens herself to the life-giving Spirit of God, in conceiving her child, and co-operates with God's gracious purpose, in the complete simplicity of faith and love: 'Be it unto me according to thy word.' In her entire openness to God, she becomes the bearer of Christ, and the channel of divine love for the world.

In accepting her calling, then, she has a special relationship to God; and in becoming the mother of Jesus she has a unique bond with her son. It is no disparagement of the father's role in child nurture, to re-affirm the ancient insight that 'mothers are the makers of spirit'. The place of the father in child development is important; that of the mother is fundamental. For the infant, in the first decisive year or two of life, the mother's love and care – or lack of them – are critical for the formation of character. Dr Frank Lake, the founder of the Clinical Theology movement, coined the suggestive phrase 'the womb of the spirit'. By that he meant that, just as the child, in the nine months prior to its birth, is biologically utterly dependent on the mother, so after birth dependence continues at an even deeper level.

The infant needs not only food and drink, warmth and shelter, which the mother supplies. The new-born also needs love and tender care, expressed through physical touch and fondling, being held, kissed, being spoken or sung to in the unmistakable tones of love. Lake stresses the importance of the child's seeing constantly the loving face of the mother, beaming down upon him. He borrows the language of the Psalmist, and speaks of the child as living in the light of the mother's countenance. The child 'knows no heaven but her face'. In so far as the mother's nurture of her child is faithfully and unselfishly accomplished, the foundations of a strong and outgoing personality will have been laid. It is a commonplace that behind every good man or woman, we shall expect to find, at the first springs of their lives, a good mother.

What then shall we say of Jesus, whose humanity is integral, whole, unflawed by self-centredness, the pattern of what men and women should be? 'Behold, the man!' When we do behold him, tempted in all ways as we are, yet without sin, we surely have to reckon with the matchless mothering which Mary gave him. We not only 'behold the man'; we 'behold the handmaid of the Lord', who, as the mother of Jesus, so faithfully carried out the divine will. Mary's *fiat* expresses her utter willingness to co-operate with God's will, and to put herself at the disposal of his loving purpose for mankind. In the shattering petition of the Lord's Prayer, mind-blowing in its implications, we ask that God's will may be done, 'on earth, as it is in heaven'. At the moment of conception, Mary does that. She plays her part in carrying out God's good and perfect will in this world, just as it is perfectly fulfilled in heaven.

Mary, then, is for believers a pattern of faith. She points us to Jesus the Lord, who is 'Mary's Son'. We may say more than that. Since Christians form the Body of Christ, then, in the deepest sense, Mary the Mother of the Lord is also – like the Jerusalem that is from above – the Mother of us all.

8

THE COMMON LIFE IN CHRIST

RED ACRE IS a large, 1920s house down a quiet road in West Kirby, on the Wirral Peninsula. It commands superb views of Deeside, Hilbre Island, and the distant mountains of North Wales. It resembles many of the detached houses thereabouts, but has two distinctive features. Within its grounds is a second, smaller house, with its own chapel. This house is home to a small religious community, named on the doorplate of the main house as 'The Sisters of Jesus' Way'.

Five women comprise the community. The local people speak of them as 'the Methodist nuns', and are not quite sure what to make of them. They are loyal Methodists, but in their spirituality they have looked beyond the walls of their own denomination. They have in fact taken much of their inspiration from the Evangelical Sisters of Mary at Darmstadt in Germany. The two senior sisters were members of the Wesley Deaconess Order (now the Methodist Diaconal Order), until they heard the call to live a life in community. They have been joined by three younger women, and their ideal remains the same: a life of simplicity, prayer, caring and outreach. The sisters' Rule of Life sets before them a vision of a house where 'there should be an atmosphere of prayer and peace, but above all of sheer happiness that Jesus has made His dwelling with us'. The sisters would never trumpet the fact, but many a visitor has found that the prayer and peace and happiness are not simply an ideal; they are visibly and palpably present at Red Acre.

The joyful spirituality is rooted in a simple life of hard work. The sisters keep open house, and may have up to seventeen people staying with them at any one time, who have to be fed and cared for. Some guests may be recovering from illness or breakdown; others are searching spiritually, trying to find God, or his way for their lives; yet others have come for rest and quiet and re-creation. The sisters, with the aid of one domestic helper and one handyman, do all the cleaning, cooking, laundering, gardening. They bake their own bread, and grow their own fruit and vegetables. They have formed a library for the use of visitors. When their community house was being built, they put in the foundations and did a lot of the labouring themselves. Their joy is certainly not the product of a life of leisured ease.

Their personal lifestyle, as sisters in community, is one of celibacy and the sharing of possessions. Their income derives mainly from gifts in money and in kind, and from part-time work. They never appeal for money, and no charges are made to their many guests. In the entrance hall there is a box where gifts may be placed 'in thankfulness for God's fatherly care', by which the sisters seek to live. No gifts are sought or canvassed. Yet the gifts come, from those who have received help and hospitality, or from those who have been impressed by a communal life of 'faith working by love'.

The community at Red Acre is, no doubt, one small example of a growing trend in Christendom. There has been a great flowering of groups and communities, both residential and dispersed. Methodists, like other Christians, have been caught up in this movement. Yet should they have been? Does the local nickname for the Sisters of Jesus Way – 'the Methodist nuns' – contain a contradiction? It would be easy to argue that the sisters' pattern of life is in fact a departure from the authentic Methodist understanding of the Christian life.

One of the Wesley hymns, it is true, might seem to give sanction for a withdrawal from the world. It falls within the section of hymns entitled 'For the Society Praying', and contains the lines:

In Jesu's name behold we meet,
Far from an evil world retreat,
   And all its frantic ways;
One only thing resolved to know,
And square our useful lives below
   By reason and by grace.

Yet the next verse makes clear that the withdrawal for prayer is only temporary. There is no question of these Methodists forming a separate community. The following lines are in fact dismissive of the monastic life, at least of the enclosed kind:

Not in the tombs we pine to dwell,
Not in the dark monastic cell,
   By vows and grates confined;
Freely to all ourselves we give,
Constrained by Jesu's love to live
   The servants of mankind.[1]

In defence of the sisters, it must be said first, that they are not an enclosed order; and second, that they are indeed 'Constrained by Jesu's love to live/The servants of mankind'. It would be hard to find a better brief description of their lifestyle. Moreover, whatever Charles Wesley's hymn may say in writing off the religious life, it seems clear that John Wesley felt the pull of its attraction.

What is the evidence for that? To glean the evidence, we need to start perhaps with John's birthplace, the remote and somewhat barbaric parish of Epworth in the Lincolnshire fens. As a small boy, Wesley could see from his home in the rectory the remains of a small Carthusian priory, one of Shakespeare's 'bare ruined quires, where late the sweet birds sang'. The Carthusians were the most austere and dedicated of orders, who resisted to the death Henry VIII's dissolution of the monasteries and breach with Rome. When John Wesley was sent away to school, it was to Charterhouse in London that he went. The school was, in the eighteenth century, still on the site of the great London house of the

97

Carthusians, from which in 1535 the Prior and brethren were taken to the Tower and thence to their brutal execution at Tyburn.[2] It is, of course, impossible to say what influence this double exposure to the physical remains of the Carthusian order may have had on the mind of the young Wesley. The conscious effect may have been minimal. Yet, in the light of his later development, it would be rash to rule out the possibility that these evidences of monasticism spoke to his growing mind.

From Charterhouse, John Wesley went up to Oxford, as a scholar of Christ Church. After graduation, he was elected a Fellow of Lincoln College, and in due course assumed the leadership of an earnest group of undergraduates already nicknamed the Holy Club. The members were bound together by a strict rule of life, which involved systematic study of the Greek Testament, devout observance of the fasts and services of the Church, private prayer, and practical works of charity. The latter included teaching the children of the poor, and visiting prisoners in Oxford gaol. Professor Albert Outler rightly describes the Holy Club as 'a small semimonastic group', and points out that the members developed a keen interest in 'the monastic piety of the fourth-century "desert fathers" '.[3] Writing over half a century later, John makes clear that he and his brother Charles both felt the same call to solitude which drew the desert fathers to the wilderness. They even considered transferring the Holy Club from Oxford to some remote and rural place, where they could pursue the quest for perfection without distraction.

Wesley was replying, in 1774, to Mary Bishop, one of his Methodist correspondents. She tells him: 'Retirement is the soil in which my soul prospers. In company my spirit seems removed from its place of rest; for which reason I go out less than ever. I do not know but love of solitude grows upon me, perhaps more than it ought.' By this date, after nearly forty years in the saddle as an itinerant preacher, Wesley had long since abandoned dreams of a solitary life of contemplation. Yet he makes clear that it was not always so with him. At Oxford, as a young don in the Holy Club, he had felt the same pull as Mary Bishop feels now. So he counsels her all the more firmly not to give way to her disposition to retire from the active life of the world:

> I think it will not be best for you to go out less than you ever did. Suppose you have more faith and more love . . . you certainly ought to go out more. Otherwise your faith will insensibly die away. It is *by works* only that it can be *made perfect*. And the more the love of solitude is indulged the more it will increase. This is a temptation common to men. In every age and country Satan has whispered to those who began to taste the powers of the age to come (as well as to Gregory Lopez), '*Au désert! Au désert!*' Most of our little flock at Oxford were tried with this, my brother and I in particular. Nay, but I say 'To the Bible! To the Bible!' And there you will learn, 'as you have time, to do good unto all men.'[4]

Yet, despite the force of his disclaimer to Miss Bishop, Wesley continued to feel the pull of the religious life, separated from 'the world'. He would on occasion look back to his quiet, ordered days in the Holy Club, and in the whirl of his activity as evangelist and reformer, cry out with Horace, 'Give me back my former life!' So, in 1772, hard-pressed with business, he writes to his brother, Charles: 'I often cry out, "*Vitae me redde priori!*" Let me be again an Oxford Methodist! I am often in doubt whether it would not be best for me to resume all my Oxford rules, great and small. I did then walk closely with God and redeem the time. But what have I been doing these thirty years?'[5]

That nostalgic heart-cry is understandable, given the relentless activity of Wesley's mature years. Whatever demands he made on his followers and helpers, he more than fulfilled himself. For the lay travelling preachers he called and trained, he drew up the 'Rules of an Assistant'. The first rule sets the tone: '1. Be diligent. Never be unemployed a moment, never be triflingly employed, never while away time; spend no more time at any place than is strictly necessary.'[6] The economy of Wesley's style reinforces his admonition to his men. He does not waste a word; they are not to fritter away a minute. It is easy to see why the patron saint of Methodism has been said to be St Vitus!

Activism, however, is not the whole story. There is a contemplative element in Methodist spirituality, which is clearly discernible in Charles Wesley's hymns. On the one side, Charles can call for ceaseless activity as forcefully as John. His haunting hymn for New Year's Day begins:

> Come, let us anew
> Our journey pursue,
>   Roll round with the year,
> And never stand still till the Master appear![7]

St Vitus holds the field. Yet the same Charles Wesley can sow the seeds of contemplation in a hymn such as 'Open, Lord, my inward ear', with its call for utter stillness and silent waiting upon God:

> From the world of sin, and noise,
>   And hurry, I withdraw;
> For the small and inward voice
>   I wait, with humble awe.
> Silent am I now, and still,
>   Dare not in thy presence move;
> To my waiting soul reveal
> The secret of thy love.[8]

J. E. Rattenbury was inclined to place this hymn among the half-dozen greatest that Charles Wesley wrote.[9] It is the prayer of a Christian mystic, or at least of Charles in a mystical vein far removed from the intense activism which was such a brandmark of early Methodism.

Yet, more typical of the Methodist ethos, and of the Wesley hymns, is Charles's determination to hold together the active and contemplative aspects of Christian living. So, in 'Holy Lamb, who thee confess', he takes Christ as the pattern for living, and addresses him thus:

> While thou didst on earth appear,
> Servant to thy servants here,
> Mindful of thy place above,
> All thy life was prayer and love.

The same must be true of Christ's followers. Prayer and action must be conjoined:

> Such our whole employment be:
> Works of faith and charity,
> Works of love on man bestowed,
> Secret intercourse with God.

Such a life contains the spring of joy. The Christian draws on the resources of grace, not for self-satisfaction, but to spend and be spent in the service of God's children.

> Vessels, instruments of grace,
> Pass we thus our happy days
> 'Twixt the mount and multitude,
> Doing or receiving good.[10]

''Twixt the mount and multitude' well expresses the attempt to hold together action and contemplation, prayer and work. Charles Wesley derives the thought from the account of Jesus and the disciples on the Mount of Transfiguration. After the vision of glory, and the exaltation, they come down to earth again. A crowd is waiting, a desperately sick boy, and all the pressure of human need closes round them once more. In modern Methodist communities there has been a real attempt to root the common life of prayer and fellowship in the midst of the 'multitude' and the needs of the inner city. That has been true, for example, both of the Wesley Community and of the Ashram Community founded by Dr John Vincent, whose radical Christianity is rooted in the Gospels.

The term *ashram* is borrowed from India, where it has long been used in Hinduism to describe a place of religious practice in community. It may also have overtones of a simpler lifestyle, a return to basics, in reaction against the sophisticated consumerism of the West. John Vincent's ashram began with a handful of like-minded people in 1967. By 1986, it numbered some eighty members, together with a much larger group of sympathizers and supporters scattered across the country. It has community houses in inner-city Sheffield, and at Sparkbrook, Birmingham.

Dr Vincent defines the Ashram Community as 'a community of disciples of Jesus Christ which seeks to provoke new calls from the Gospel, enable new ventures of faith, support new enterprises in service, experiment with new ways of action, have as much as possible in common, pioneer action in politics, discover and stand beside those in need, provide alternative models for the churches'.

Though an avowedly Christian community, it adopts an open-door policy, and is accessible 'to all who desire to commit themselves to the Community and its way of life'. Methodist in inspiration, it is ecumenical in spirit and practice. The Ashram Community has a strong sense of the new wine of the gospel, of Jesus as radical innovator, who challenges the norms of our society, as he did those of the first century. It takes seriously the message of Jesus and the coming of the Kingdom as 'good news for the poor' (Luke 4.18). With its Methodist roots, it seeks to obey John Wesley's injunction to his preachers and people to go, 'not only to those who need you, but to those who need you most'.

Hence the Sparkbrook Community House in inner-city Birmingham is in one of the most deprived parts of Britain. Its members see their calling as a strenuously active and committed one: 'to be an active body of Christians working for local change; listening and responding to needs in our multi-racial, multi-faith neighbourhood'. In practical terms, that has meant: employment creation, advice, a home repairs project, the formation of a Credit Union, and creating volunteering and employment opportunities for long-term unemployed people. The life of the Community is rooted in worship. At the same time, it remains intensely down-to-earth, and one might apply to the ashrams the admiring description once given to the Salvation Army, as 'Christianity with its sleeves rolled up'.[11]

So far, so activist, it may seem. There are, however, other communities which have sprung up in Methodism which are more contemplative in ethos and style. One such is the Wesley Community, formed by Dr Ronald Gibbins and his wife Olive in 1978. Dr Gibbins was then minister of Wesley's Chapel in the City Road, London, which was re-opened that year after extensive renovation. The rededication service took place two centuries to the day from the original opening of the church, and prompted a vision of the future, as well as thanksgiving for the past. As a member of the Methodist Sacramental Fellowship, Dr Gibbins was committed to a life of ordered devotion, centred in the Eucharist and expressed in outreach and caring in the local community. The stated aims of the Community combine the ideals of depth of spirituality and breadth of outreach in language which owes much to John Wesley's own:

1. To strive for perfection in the growth of our spiritual life and help others to do this;
2. To reach out to the world in every way possible to do all the good we can by all the means we can.

The Community is organized in local Chapters, and in 1989 there were Chapters in the Methodist East End Mission, in Stockwell, and in Edinburgh. Each Chapter consists of a small group of Christians, mainly but not exclusively Methodist, who live together, share a common rule of life and worship, and support themselves financially. A Chapter is linked to its local Methodist church, and committed to supporting its life and work. To emphasize this integral connexion, and in true Wesleyan spirit, the Guidelines of the Community lay down the principle that 'each Chapter lives under the direction of the Superintendent Minister of the Methodist Circuit where it is located'. The Community has its own book of Daily Offices, containing orders for Morning and Evening Prayer and for Compline.

Both the Christian Ashram and the Wesley Community are attempts to combine a common life of prayer with active service of the community. Both aspire to live out their common life 'twixt the mount and multitude'. Yet, clearly, they cannot be a model for the great majority of Christians. For most, ties of family and work preclude living together in a common house with its own rule of life. Yet the communities do impinge on the lives of other Christians in significant ways. First, by their very existence, they underline the need for balance in the Christian life. Prayer and service, contemplation and action, the mount and the multitude, need to be integrated in the life of faith. The communities show various ways in which that may be done.

As we have seen, there is a strongly activist bias to Methodism. Indeed, Evangelical Protestants generally have tended to major on an active, strenuous life of service – despite all their traditional warnings against justification by works. Within the broader Protestant tradition, perhaps the Quakers have formed the most decisive counterweight to this lopsided piety. The Society of Friends has never been backward in good works. Yet at the same time, its members have witnessed to the place of silence, stillness and contemplation in the life of the believer. Many of the modern religious communities have reinforced that lesson, and have helped to provide 'space' for those who want to take it seriously.

The help has normally taken two forms. First, a number of residential communities have encouraged other Christians to become associates. When I ministered in the West London Mission, some of the women members of my congregation were associates of the St Julian's Community, near Horsham in Sussex. They accepted a discipline of prayer which linked them to the community. From time to time, they went down to Sussex to spend a few days at the community house, sharing in its corporate life of prayer. It was not an exercise in pietist escapism by people who could not face the real world. These were women heavily committed in their working life and in service of church and community. The brief withdrawal for a weekend at St Julian's was a recharging of the batteries, and they came back to London renewed and refreshed.

The same pattern has spread more widely through a

second service the residential communities have offered. They have opened their doors to those who are neither members nor associates, but have asked for a Quiet Day or a period of retreat. The growth of the Retreat Movement is one of the more striking developments in British Christianity in the last quarter-century. Understandably, it has not been trumpeted abroad like the many movements for renewal and evangelism. Nevertheless, its quiet growth has been impressive. The magazine *Vision* is the organ of the Association for Promoting Retreats, and its contents are revealing. The 1993 edition of this annual publication lists over 170 retreat houses in Britain and Ireland, ranging from Buckfast Abbey, Devon, to the House of the Resurrection at Mirfield, West Yorkshire.

The retreat centres are not only widely diverse in type and location. They also offer a most variegated fare to the would-be retreatant. Take, for instance, the Othona Community at Burton Bradstock, Dorset. Its 1993 programme included a contemplative retreat, following, no doubt, a traditional pattern of brief talks and directed silence. Another week was devoted to 'Word and Image: an exploration of the power of symbols in literature, painting, worship, dreams and ordinary life'. Also on offer was a week given over to 'The Poetry of Meditation – with particular reference to T. S. Eliot, Edwin Muir, Kathleen Raine and R. S. Thomas'. Another retreat on 'Calligraphy and Prayer' might well claim resonance with Benedictine spirituality, in which prayer is work – the *opus Dei* – and work is prayer.

It may be objected that these new patterns of retreat are simply a sugaring of the pill of prayer and worship to make them more acceptable to the modern palate. Maybe; but there is no necessity to conclude that that is so. Rather, I believe there is here a genuine attempt to explore the rich resources available, in literature, art and craft, for spirituality and the life of faith.

In both the modern Christian communities and the Retreat Movement, there are many resonances across the lines of denomination and tradition. Both provide fruitful fields for spiritual ecumenism. The 1993 issue of *Vision* contained an article by Margaret Jarman, who chairs the Baptist Retreat Group. She has recently had to discontinue her active ministry, owing to the onset of ME. Out of this experience, she writes about trusting in the darkness. Here she has found great help, not only from Luther, but from St John of the Cross, with his reflections on the Dark Night of the Soul. She writes: 'Some people from my own evangelical tradition find it hard to understand that I am helped by someone like John of the Cross. Yet his teaching enriches my own spiritual roots.'[12]

In the same issue, the Methodist Retreat Group announced that its annual retreat would take place at Launde Abbey, the retreat house of the Anglican Diocese of Leicester. The leader of the retreat was to be Bishop Kallistos Ware of the Greek Orthodox Church in Great Britain. The confluence of spiritual traditions – Orthodox, Anglican, Methodist – represented in that gathering would once have been a nine-days' wonder. Not any more. Now it is quite typical, part of the ecumenical 'God's plenty' available to Christians. Heart speaks to heart, and finds an answer so often from the most unlikely source. We may see it as part of the sovereign freemasonry of the Spirit.

9

ONE IN THE SPIRIT:
THE CHARISMATIC MOVEMENT AND
THE CHURCHES

JOHN WESLEY, AS he preached up and down the country
in the open air, ran into a barrage of criticism. Many
disliked his message. Others objected to his preaching in
other clergymen's parishes without so much as by-your-leave.
To this charge, Wesley replied somewhat pontifically, 'I look
upon the whole world as my parish.'

Something of Wesley's world vision rubbed off on his
Methodist people, who, through their official Conference,
annually elect a President to lead them. The President has
not only to visit the churches throughout Britain, but also
to carry out a little parochial visitation on a global scale.

It was in the course of these duties that I found myself, in
the August of 1981, in Singapore, *en route* for Sri Lanka.
Trinity College, Singapore, had laid on a refresher course
for Chinese and Malay ministers from across the Protestant
churches. My contribution was to give a short course of
lectures on pastoral theology. Lectures and discussion occupied the mornings and afternoons, but evenings were normally free. Dr and Mrs Ted Newing, Australian Anglicans,
were our hosts. My wife and I knew them well, from the days
when we had been colleagues together on the staff of St
Paul's United Theological College in Limuru, Kenya. The
Newings were determined to let us see something of the
varied and exotic life of Singapore. They took us to an
orchid farm, gave us a beach picnic, and one evening treated
us to dinner at the celebrated Raffles Hotel. As a throw-back
to the palmy days of the Empire, the Raffles had its own

fascination. Yet equally absorbing, in a quite different way, was an evening spent at the college.

The staff had arranged a set-piece debate on the impact of the Charismatic Renewal Movement on the life of the Singaporean churches. I had been invited to attend, but had no part in the debate. Having done more than my share of speaking during the week, I was quite content to be simply a fly on the wall. In both England and Kenya, I had found Charismatic Renewal could be an inflammatory issue. I was curious to know what the ministers of Singapore would make of it. Curiosity was amply rewarded. The spirited debate revealed passionately held differences within the city's broadly Protestant-Evangelical churches. The proposer of the motion welcoming the Charismatic Movement was a professor of medicine from the University of Singapore. He was a senior academic, but interestingly was about to resign his chair in order to undertake full-time preaching and evangelistic work. Opposing him was a middle-aged Presbyterian minister, who claimed that his large congregation had been bitterly divided by the Charismatic Movement. He contended that the movement had seriously harmed the life of the Church, and that its theology was badly defective, its understanding of the Holy Spirit distorted, its interpretation of Scripture one-sided and misleading; its baleful effect on the life of a congregation was to create two categories of Christians, first- and second-class, according to their experience of the Spirit. Both positions were well argued, and it was clear to a visitor that here was a substantial rift in the life of the Church.

The debate was revealing in other ways too. It showed clearly that the Charismatic Movement had long since burst the bounds of its American and European beginnings. It had spread throughout Wesley's world parish. The fact that the champion of the movement in the Singapore debate was a lay person was significant also. Though clergy and religious had been drawn into it, the movement began with lay people and has kept a strong lay identity. The debate further demonstrated how fiercely the movement is able to polarize Christians, even where they share a common Evangelical faith. Those who upheld the claims of the Spirit had been met head-on by those who championed the sovereignty of the written Word. That conflict is an old one. It agitated some of the Puritans and early Quakers, as Dr Geoffrey Nuttall showed so convincingly in his outstanding study of *The Holy Spirit in Puritan Faith and Experience* (1946).

However, it is certainly no knock-down argument against the Charismatic Movement to object that it has divisive effects. So have most movements of Christian renewal, certainly in their initial stages, and often long after. Early Methodism was intensely controversial, as indeed was original Christianity. You may applaud the Charismatic Movement, or abominate it. You may prefer to give it discriminating appraisal, and try to separate the wheat from the chaff. What you cannot justly do, in surveying contemporary Christianity, is ignore it. It is now a world-wide movement, with adherents in all the major Christian Churches, who in 1983 were estimated at eleven million people. They include theologians, members of religious orders, and representatives of the hierarchy of the Churches. The figure of eleven million is taken from Dr Gordon Wakefield's *A Dictionary of Christian Spirituality,* (1983), which devotes a major article to 'The Charismatic Movement'. The author of the article is Quentin Lister, a Dominican scholar, who writes from within the movement. He was in 1983 the professor of theology at the Pontifical University of St Thomas Aquinas in Rome. He shows how seriously Rome has taken the Charismatic Movement and the classical Pentecostalism to which it relates. Since 1972, the Vatican has held annual theological conversations with representatives of both the old and new Pentecostalism, from which a measure of mutual understanding has flowed. In 1975, Pope Paul VI received 10,000 charismatics in Rome, thanks largely to the good offices of the Belgian Cardinal Suenens, whose whole ministry has been reshaped by the charismatic renewal.

The movement, then, has spread impressively across the world since its beginning in the early 1960s. It has been strikingly successful in bridging the Catholic-Protestant divide. One of the memorable features of the Nationwide Initiative in Evangelism conference at Nottingham in 1980 was the unity in diversity which the charismatics displayed. Members of House Churches, old-style Pentecostals, Evangelicals of all stripes, together with Catholic religious (Franciscan, Dominican, Benedictine), shared in early morning prayer and praise meetings with great freedom and oneness in the Spirit. Clearly, the Charismatic Movement has had a significant impact on the life of the Christian churches. But what does it signify? Has it depth as well as breadth?

To answer that question, I would go back to a book published before the modern Charismatic Movement had even begun. In 1953, Lesslie Newbigin, then Bishop in Madurai, a diocese of the recently united Church of South India, published his Kerr Lectures under the title of *The Household of God: Lectures on the Nature of the Church*. It has proved to be an extraordinarily prophetic book. In it Bishop Newbigin identified three essential forms of Christian faith and life. The Protestant form characterized the Church as 'The Congregation of the Faithful'. The Catholic form saw the Church as essentially 'The Body of Christ'. The third form he identified as the Pentecostal, which celebrated the Church as 'The Community of the Holy Spirit'. I read the book when it was first published, and was frankly amazed at the prominence Newbigin gave to the Pentecostal form. Surely he was exaggerating when he set that alongside the mainstream Catholic and Protestant types of the Church? Perhaps he had been led astray by a desire to develop his thesis along schematic Trinitarian lines? Whatever his reasoning, I was quite unconvinced. Yet now, forty years on from the publication of *The Household of God*, it is my misgivings which are dated, not Lesslie Newbigin's thesis.

Marcus Ward, the Methodist ecumenist and colleague of Bishop Newbigin in the Church of South India, had grasped the significance of the Charismatic Movement as early as 1966. In February of that year, he wrote to the Anglican mystic, Marjorie Milne:

What you say about your discovery of the Pentecostalists is intensely interesting to me. In some small way I have found what you have been finding, more indeed in other lands than in this. I wonder whether you talked about it when you were with the Newbigins? One of the great things about his *Household of God* is the recognition (and he has been the first in the 'going concern' to see it) that the Pentecostalists represent not a deviation but a true dimension.[1]

Lesslie Newbigin's pioneering study sought to do justice to that dimension. It is a commonplace that the Holy Spirit has been the most neglected Person of the Trinity in much Christian teaching. Yet, as Newbigin points out, 'The Holy Spirit may be the last article of the Creed but in the New Testament it is the first fact of experience.'[2] The Charismatic Movement has brought an overwhelming emphasis on the person, gifts, fruit and renewing power of the Spirit.

It is the experiential factor which is so vital here. The great doctrines of the Faith need to be internalized in the heart and life of the believer. Luther never tired of insisting that 'It is not enough that Christ was born in Bethlehem; he must be born in *you*.' Similarly, Malcolm Stewart, in a contemporary Christian song on the Resurrection, makes the point that, '... today the only stone that rolls away to let him live is – *inside you*'. Hence Newbigin characterizes the Pentecostal stream of the Church's life as having as its central conviction, 'that the Christian life is a matter of the experienced power and presence of the Holy Spirit today'. It follows from that conviction that 'neither orthodoxy of doctrine nor impeccability of succession can take the place of this; that an excessive emphasis upon those immutable elements of the Gospel upon which orthodox Catholicism and Protestantism have concentrated attention may, and often in fact does, result in a Church which is a mere shell, having the form of a church but not the life'.[3]

To speak seriously of the Spirit – that is, God within us – is inevitably to be concerned with Christian experience at a profoundly personal level. The Charismatic Movement has

111

undoubtedly brought many people to a new, or renewed, experience of the love of God in Jesus Christ, present through the power of the Spirit. Many Christians in the West, with its strongly rational and intellectual approach to religion, have found this experiential Christianity as refreshing as rain after drought. This discovery of a deeper, personal dimension of faith has been particularly striking among Roman Catholics. They have had the benefits of a strong, clear and consistent teaching authority. They have been upheld by a firm system of sacramental grace. They have had instilled into them from childhood the importance of fulfilling the external duties of religion. Admittedly, instructed Catholics will also have been left in no doubt that the practice of the Christian faith is far more than a matter of externals. Sincerity of heart and mind, and the translation of faith into a life of goodness – these are indispensable. Yet in practice, if we listen to Catholic Pentecostalists, it has been easy for some to carry out all the outward duties of faith, and yet lack its inner light and fire.

Kristina Cooper, a journalist who edits *Good News*, the newsletter of the Catholic Charismatic Renewal in England, may be taken as typical of many Catholics who have made this particular pilgrimage of faith. Her contribution to a recent series on 'How I pray', in *The Tablet*, begins:

> Although I have always been a practising Catholic, I did not really start to pray until I had a conversion experience while working as a volunteer for the Church in Panama. Before that, prayer was saying an 'Our Father' and a 'Hail Mary' on my knees next to my bed before I went to sleep, and going to Mass on a Sunday. God was very far away. It was almost as if he inhabited another planet, and so prayer was something I did out of respect and habit because he was God, without really knowing why I did it.

Then she was invited to join a charismatic prayer group, and did so reluctantly. Yet she found that these ordinary folk 'seemed to have an intimacy with God that I had never experienced, despite all the soup runs and other good works

112

I had done'. Through the influence of this small group of Catholics, she entered into a quite new experience of faith. God became for her, 'real and huge and powerful and cared for me in a personal way'.

The essential point to grasp here, it seems to me, is that all this happened to her within the fellowship of the Catholic Church. Though at some points she may write like a Protestant, she had no need to become one. She had found this new fullness of personal faith within her own communion. One of the immediate results of her 'baptism in the Spirit' was to give her a hunger for the Scriptures. No Protestant could outdo her zeal to drink at this inexhaustible well: 'I just could not put the Bible down. It suddenly became more exciting than the most compulsive thriller.' She has in fact adopted a scheme of Bible reading which takes her through the whole of the Scriptures annually. Yet at the same time, her Bible reading has not replaced her devotion to the sacraments. Quite the reverse; for the last ten years she has attended Mass almost daily. Moreover she has consciously linked her love and knowledge of the Bible to her regular sacramental worship: 'I read the Mass readings of the day and look at the daily meditations in *Word Among Us*, a Catholic scripture magazine. I do this to prepare myself for Mass, because I easily become distracted and float in and out of the celebration when I am there.'[4]

Lest it be thought that Kristina Cooper's reactions are untypical and merely personal to herself, we may call in evidence Cardinal Suenens, one of the leaders of the Catholic movement of Charismatic Renewal. Leo Joseph Suenens, now in his eighty-ninth year, was a Moderator of the Second Vatican Council. He was Archbishop of Malines-Brussels 1961–79, and raised to the cardinalate in 1962. He has written extensively, both on ecumenism and on the Charismatic Movement. In 1971 he co-edited with Archbishop Michael Ramsey *The Future of the Christian Church*. When he writes on the Charismatic Renewal Movement, he does so from within, passionately committed to it both as theologian and church leader. He sees it not as a fringe development, but as central to the life and mission of the whole Church. Though his book, *A New Pentecost?* carried a question mark in the title, in deference to the sceptics, he himself is in no doubt at all that the pentecostal movement is a divine gift to the Church.

Writing quite independently, in an earlier issue of the same journal as Kristina Cooper, Cardinal Suenens strikes the same chords as she does. He writes, naturally, with more theological sophistication, but he describes the same experience of renewal. Writing in 1992, the twenty-fifth anniversary of the Second Vatican Council, he is concerned, as was the Council, with the renewal of the life of the Church. That Council began 'a necessary and as yet incomplete revision of its [the Church's] structure'. Now a deeper renewal is called for, one directed towards 'the very foundations of the faith'. Then, in a remarkable passage, which might have come from the pen of a Protestant evangelist, the Cardinal insists:

> Christians today have to rediscover the heart of the Christian message; they have been sufficiently 'sacramentalised'; they have not been sufficiently 'evangelised'. We are now faced with the task of rediscovering and explaining what really makes a Christian. We must help Christians to become more continually aware of their faith and to live it on a more personal level. Many must exchange a sociological or an inherited Christianity for a full and active life of faith, based on a personal decision and embraced with full consciousness.[5]

Urging that the charismatic renewal constitutes 'an answer' – not *the* answer – 'to the questions now facing the Church', he looks at the personal experience of those who have been 'renewed in the Holy Spirit'. He finds 'several constant elements that favour the transformation of passive Christians into active ones'.

First, such Christians find themselves challenged by the New Testament witness to the power and gifts of the Spirit in the lives of the first believers. Was such power simply a jump-start given to the early Church, or is it the permanent driving-force of the Christian community? In Suenens' words, 'Were those Christians of the early Church exceptional, or is it that we Christians of today, with our weakened faith, are really sub-normal?' He himself is clear that the Pentecostal gifts are as available for today's Church as they were for the first-century one.

A second element of the renewal is its spiritual democracy. A life transformed by the Spirit is not meant for a few specialists in sanctity. It is for all God's people. All are 'called to be saints'. In the Cardinal's words: 'the manifestations of the Spirit are found among Christians of every walk of life. These are not hermits or 'specialists' in search of sanctity; these are rank and file Christians.'

The third element which Suenens singles out from the renewal experience is the personal encounter with Jesus which the Spirit brings about. 'A Christian is a changed person, a convert: he has turned away from himself, so as to adhere to Jesus of Nazareth who, for his sake, died and rose from the dead.' Those renewed by the Spirit have 'made a personal discovery of Jesus'. A Christian is defined as 'someone who has met Jesus as the one who "baptises in the Holy Spirit" '.[6]

The language the Cardinal uses here would be perfectly acceptable to many Protestant Evangelicals. It may indeed give the impression at times that Catholic Pentecostals have succumbed to the more individualistic emphases of popular Protestantism. Against that, we must set the profound effect which the new Pentecostalism has had on corporate Christian worship. This influence has spread far beyond the bounds of the Charismatic Movement itself, as a glance at recent hymn books of the mainstream churches will indicate. The Charismatic Movement has for many Christians brought a new warmth and spontaneity to worship. Here again, perhaps unwittingly, it reminds us of the apostolic Church. The early Christian Church enjoyed a richly varied pattern of worship, which combined set liturgical forms (psalms, prayers, responses), drawn from the synagogue, with free forms of prayer and praise. In the modern Christian West, these two traditions have often drawn apart, to the impoverishment of both. Extempore prayer, moreover, can become just as hidebound as the most fixed liturgical form. Both need the quickening breath of the Spirit, and the 'vital piety' the Spirit inspires, to animate them. In its openness to the Spirit in worship, the Charismatic Movement has shown itself a channel through which a renewing stream of life and joy has flowed into the corporate praise of the Churches.

It is remarkable how the worship patterns of the Charismatic Movement have permeated the life of the mainstream Churches. Ecumenical worship can sometimes be rather bland. If we take out the sharp, distinctive flavours of our separate traditions, we may be left with a liturgical dish with little tang or bite to it, and which, in an effort to please all tastes, satisfies none. Yet in our ecumenical worship on Merseyside, I do not believe that the liturgical salt has lost its savour. In January 1993, for example, Roman Catholics, Anglicans and Free Church Christians gathered for a united service in the Week of Prayer for Christian Unity. We met in the Roman Catholic Church of St Patrick, Wigan, for a service devised to express the set theme for the year, 'Be fruitful in the Spirit'. The liturgy was spiced with flavour from some of the liveliest traditions of contemporary Christian worship. The hymn which led into the Scripture readings was from the Iona Community, and sung to the tune of the Skye Boat Song:

> Spirit of God, as strong as the wind,
> Gentle as is the dove,
> Give us your joy and give us your peace,
> Show to us Jesus' love.

The *Gloria* and *Kyrie* were taken from the Taizé Community, and were sung with great vigour, being now so well known across the Churches. The opening hymn came from the stream of charismatic piety within the English-speaking world, again so familiar to Christians generally that they may forget its source and origin:

Jesus is Lord!
Creation's voice proclaims it,
for by his power each tree and flower
was planned and made . . .

Its chorus underlines the Christ-centred devotion of the Pentecostal renewal:

Jesus is Lord! Jesus is Lord!
Praise him with 'Hallelujahs',
for Jesus is Lord!

The Charismatic Movement has encouraged the whole Christian people to 'praise him with Hallelujahs', and they have on the whole readily responded to the invitation.

One of the high moments of the service was the sharing of the Peace. It was introduced by the one leading worship with the words:

The fruit of the Spirit is love, joy and peace.
If we live in the Spirit, let us walk in the Spirit.
The peace of the Lord be always with you.

The answering response, 'And also with you' was the signal for all heaven to break loose, in what is sometimes colloqui-ally referred to as a 'hubbub peace'. The congregation cheerfully broke ranks to exchange the ancient Christian 'kiss of peace'. For some it was literally a kiss, an embrace, a warm hug. For others, it took the form of a handclasp and a word of greeting. The Church leaders were among those who exchanged hugs with their colleagues. Thirty years ago, it would probably have been unthinkable. Today, the warmth and spontaneity are taken for granted. What has caused the loosening up, the freeing of public worship in this way?

I believe the Charismatic Renewal Movement, with its stress on freedom in the Spirit, has certainly been one sig-nificant cause. It may be argued, of course, that there has been a great increase in informality in society at large. Much

117

of the starchiness has gone out of normal social intercourse. The image of the stiff-upper-lip Englishman, with his emotions as tightly fastened up as his furled umbrella, was never the whole truth. It bore some relation to reality in the upper reaches of society when the British Empire was at the zenith of its power. Yet historically, as a generalization about a whole people, it is highly suspect. For one thing, it excludes women. It also distorts the character of men. Whatever may have been true of the Victorian period, Englishmen in previous centuries freely expressed their emotions, and were not despised for doing so. The so-called 'taboo on tenderness' is a plant of much more recent growth. Richard Baxter (1615–91), the great Puritan divine, was often moved to tears as he preached, and was thought no worse of for doing so. He was in a sense doing no more than follow his own advice to preachers: 'Look on your congregation, believingly and with compassion.'

So the springs of deep feeling were there, repressed historically for a period, but ready to be released. In society at large, the 1960s saw the beginning of a trend towards greater personal freedom and self-expression. From a Christian point of view, some of that was gain; but by no means all. Along with greater self-expression went a growing moral laxity, and a decline in standards of courtesy and consideration. These elements could and did create a moral backlash among Christians, reinforcing the traditional conservatism of the Churches as institutions. The backlash never attained the scale of the American 'moral majority'; but it needed a strong countervailing force if Christian life and worship were to find greater freedom and spontaneity. A significant part of that force has been provided by the Charismatic Movement in the widest sense.

That movement has certainly permeated, through its hymns and songs, the worship of the mainstream Churches. On Merseyside, our ecumenical services regularly include hymns like 'Spirit of the living God, fall afresh on me'; 'Shine, Jesus, shine'; and 'Seek ye first the Kingdom of God'. Commonly, at a great ecumenical celebration, or the signing of a covenant by a group of local churches, we will end the service by singing

> Bind us together, Lord,
> Bind us together
> With cords that cannot be broken;
> Bind us together, Lord,
> Bind us together,
> O bind us together with love.

The practice has grown up quite spontaneously that, as we sing these words, the great congregation will join hands, along the pews and across the aisles, to give physical expression to our commitment to one another in Christ. As the people sing, with linked hands, they will often sway in time with the music. The church leaders in the sanctuary do the same, and the sense of joy and exuberance which mark the celebration is quite palpable. Those Christians whose piety has been consciously shaped by the Charismatic Movement will often raise their hands in joy during the singing of other hymns. Yet the singing of 'Bind us together, Lord' points to the wider influence of the movement. The few who raise their hands are not isolated any more. It would be untrue to claim that we are all charismatics now. It would be equally false to deny the marked influence of charismatic devotion on the hymnody and worship of the Church at large. It is surely significant that the compilers of *Hymns and Psalms* made it their aim to produce a book which should make available to all Christians 'the riches of classical, evangelical, catholic, and *charismatic* hymnody of the past and the present'.[7] That stated aim acknowledged both that charismatic hymnody is a new and distinct form of Christian praise, and that it is capable of enriching the worship of the whole Church.

Hymns and Psalms makes quite liberal use of charismatic songs and hymns, though not particularly in the section devoted to the Holy Spirit. Apart from Daniel Iverson's 'Spirit of the living God, fall afresh on me', the hymns on the Spirit are not by modern charismatic authors. They are either classics from the seventeenth to the nineteenth centuries, or modern hymns by writers who do not stand in the charismatic tradition. Canon Alan Luff, for example, has drawn on Joel and other biblical authors for his 'I will pour out my Spirit on all flesh/Your sons and your daughters shall prophesy . . .' Or again Brian Wren, one of the most felicitous of modern hymn-writers, has produced

> There's a spirit in the air,
> Telling Christians everywhere:
> Praise the love that Christ revealed,
> Living, working in our world.[8]

Yet, though there are few 'charismatic hymns' in the section on the Spirit, the number and variety of modern contributions suggests that the Charismatic Movement has in fact infiltrated the worshipping life of the mainstream Churches to an extent they have hardly realized.

The hymns from the Charismatic Movement are, significantly, found scattered throughout *Hymns and Psalms*. They include Don Fishel's 'Alleluia, alleluia, give thanks to the risen Lord'; the anonymous 'Give me joy in my heart, keep me praising'; and 'He is Lord, He is Lord,/ He is risen from the dead and He is Lord'. The charismatic hymns combine simple words with strong and joyful tunes. They use repetition and choruses, and are very easily remembered. They express an exuberance and a confidence not always found in the rather tired and tentative Churches of the West. Taken alone, they would constitute rather thin gruel; but as an admixture in the Church's full diet of worship, they bring their own refreshment. They have undoubtedly brought new warmth and joy and vitality to many congregations.

If Pentecostalism has increasingly made its influence felt in the mainstream Churches, then as Euclid would say, the converse is also true. Many classical Pentecostalists have found, in unexpected ways, that the Spirit really does blow where he wills. They in their turn have been touched and changed by the spirituality of the older Churches of Christendom. Take, for example, their attitude to Christian

120

social action. When I was in my first circuit appointment, in the early 1960s, I had some limited contact with the local Elim Pentecostal pastor. He gave me copies of a magazine which featured accounts of Pentecostal missionary work in Latin America. The reports focused on evangelism, preaching, personal conversions, the building of new congregations. They also gloried in the fact that all monies given in aid of such missionary work would be devoted solely to 'the work of the Gospel'. Not a penny would be spent on schools, hospitals, welfare, or the relief of poverty. Evangelism must be kept untainted from all such 'social gospel' activity.

The Pentecostal outlook is very different today. While no doubt pietism still reigns in some quarters, we can point to significant change, both in theology and in action. There is no need to go as far as Latin America to see the change in action. On Merseyside, the Wirral Christian Fellowship, led by its pastor, Paul Epton, is a prime example of how far change has gone. It is highly regarded in the community for its commitment to social needs. Its actions clearly demonstrate that it is in the business of 'whole salvation' rather than merely 'soul salvation'. This lively Pentecostal church is responsible for a nursery school, sheltered housing for the elderly, and a hospital for long-term mentally and physically handicapped patients. Moreover, having initially kept itself somewhat aloof from the older churches, it has now set up an ecumenical committee of reference and seeks to build bridges between its own work and that of the wider Christian movement.

It would be wrong to imply that there is a major confluence of the ecumenical and charismatic movements taking place now. On the other hand, there are scattered signs of a rapprochement. When Churches Together in Luton was formally inaugurated on 11th October 1990, some fifty-five congregations came together, drawn from right across the Christian spectrum. Among them was an Elim Pentecostal church, whose young pastor was not only one of the most enthusiastic supporters of the newly-formed ecumenical body, but its Vice-President. As far back as the 1960s, attempts were made to draw ecumenists and charismatics together, though at first with meagre results. Nevertheless, however stony the ground, seeds were sown, some of which are just beginning to bear fruit.

At the Uppsala Assembly of the World Council of Churches in 1968, a Pentecostal theologian was invited as one of the main speakers. Professor Walter Hollenweger, in his definitive study, *The Pentecostals* (1969) took as his aim the enabling of 'the Pentecostal movement and ecumenical movement to get to know each other better'.[9] He was clear that both movements had as their aim, 'to renew the Church from within'. There has certainly been a growing overlap in membership between these two agencies of Christian renewal. Nor have those who have combined charismatic and ecumenical commitment been marginal figures. If Cardinal Suenens may be taken as a leading Roman Catholic exemplar, then in David J. Du Plessis, the Pentecostalists produced an ecumenist of world stature. He served for many years as General Secretary of the World Pentecostal Conferences, and worked consistently to foster ecumenical contacts and to share the Pentecostal experience with the traditional Churches. 'He reports', according to Professor Hollenweger, 'a steadily increasing interest in the baptism of the Spirit, not within fundamentalist churches and communities, but in the liberal churches and the member churches of the World Council.'[10]

If some Pentecostalists have discovered ecumenism, numbers of Roman Catholics – committed to ecumenism by the Second Vatican Council – have entered quite deeply into the charismatic experience. That experience has, for some, not only altered and enriched their life of prayer and worship; it has also affected their theology. Since 1978, there has been held in England an annual charismatic retreat for Catholic bishops, priests and deacons. In 1993 the retreat's preacher was the Italian Capuchin friar, Father Raniero Cantalamessa. He has the gift of tongues, in that he is master of many languages. He also possesses impeccable Catholic credentials, in that he has served as official preacher to the papal household for the last fourteen years. This year, he expounded Paul's Letter to the Romans, taking as his theme 'the Lordship of Christ in the life of the Christian'. *The Tablet*'s summary of his teaching is suggestive of the measure in which his charismatic experience has led him to place a new emphasis on personal faith in appropriating the gift and promise of the Gospel:

> In his talks he urged the priests to rediscover the revelation of what being justified by faith really meant for them personally, and restore this message to their preaching. He explained how in reaction to the Reformation, the Catholic Church had tended to emphasise works without really proclaiming the good news of salvation by faith. This meant that people were often left with the impression that they had to earn their way to heaven by good works, rather than that salvation was a free gift, with works a sign of the Holy Spirit in a person's life, not a way to earn grace.[11]

David Du Plessis could hardly have put it better.

Moreover, Catholic charismatics have managed in the main to preserve a wholeness and balance in their spirituality, which the wider Pentecostal movement has sometimes lacked. Catholics have shared in the specifically Pentecostal gifts of glossolalia, prophecy and healing. Yet their charismatic commitment has also led them into community commitment, teaching, ecumenical outreach, and social action. They have not disparaged reason or the intellectual life – witness the growth of Catholic Pentecostalism in American universities like Duquesne, Notre Dame and Michigan. They would endorse John Wesley's dictum that 'all irrational religion is false religion'. Charismatic piety can at times be divisive, over-emotional, narrow in interpretation of Scripture. Yet it has shown a remarkable capacity to permeate the mainstream Churches, and to be a force for Christian renewal. At its best, it can certainly stand the test of fruits. If some have magnified the gift of tongues out of all proportion, a far greater number would endorse St Paul's confession, in 1 Corinthians 13:1; 'If I speak in the tongues of men and of angels, but have not love, I am a noisy gong or a clanging cymbal' (RSV). They would approve the warning given to his followers by John Wesley, that

> Another ground of these and a thousand mistakes, is the not considering deeply that love is the highest gift of God – humble, gentle, patient love; that all visions, revelations, manifestations whatever, are little things compared to love . . . You are to aim at nothing more, but more of that love described in the thirteenth of Corinthians. You can go no higher than this till you are carried into Abraham's bosom.[12]

EPILOGUE

As I have re-read the studies of this short book, I realize that in writing them I have only dipped my feet into a very deep river. There is so much more to be said. The recent death of John Todd, the Roman Catholic theologian, is a reminder of how recent a growth is ecumenical biography. By ecumenical biography I mean the careful, sympathetic study of the life of a leading Christian by a scholar whose allegiance is to a quite different communion within the Church of Christ.

John Todd's lives of Luther and Wesley were significant in their own right, as pieces of historical scholarship. They had an added dimension as the work of a Roman Catholic. There had, of course, been numerous Catholic studies of both reformers before Todd wrote. Yet for the most part the earlier writings had been intended to show how far the Protestants were from the truth. Their authors wanted above all to warn the faithful, to confute error, to demonstrate beyond cavil the rightness of the Catholic cause. John Todd wrote in order to understand Luther and Wesley, as men and as believers. He wrote not only with learning, but with empathy and compassion. He did not shirk controversial issues, but he showed how much common Christian truth these men shared with Roman Catholics. One can only hope that we shall see many more such studies, written across denominational lines, and with a similar integrity.

In the same way, these studies in ecumenical spirituality represent a small offering in a field where there is still so much to be done. The Christians who figure in these pages form a motley group, often widely separated in time and

125

place and culture. What on earth have Billy Bray the Cornish tin-miner and St Seraphim of Sarov in common? Or Edward King and Johann Michael Sailer? Or the Methodist Marcus Ward and the Jesuit Fathers of Heythrop College? The answer, of course, is Christ, and a whole stream of Christian life – prayer, Scripture, sacraments – which mediates Christ to his people. Surely, it may be said, we should expect to find family likenesses and resonances of the Spirit, where there is such a common pedigree? The question is plausible enough, and it has truth in it. Yet it ignores the fact that the centuries, and human wilfulness, have led to profound estrangements among Christians, and to radical separation of their traditions of life and faith.

We ought not to glamorize the ecumenical movement of the twentieth century. It is pock-marked by inconsistencies and faint-heartedness. It is a pilgrimage that in many ways has hardly yet begun. For all that, it has changed the atmosphere and altered the landscape of the Christian world. It has opened many doors, and broken down some at least of the dividing walls. 'In my Father's house are many rooms,' the Lord promises us. If that is true of the heavenly home, it is also true of Christ's Church on earth. But in the earthly house, so many of the rooms have been locked for centuries, not so much against outsiders, as against Christians of a different stripe. Mercifully, in our day the Spirit has oiled the rusty locks, and doors have begun to open.

We have begun to peer tentatively through the open doors and discover something of each other's treasures. Not everything we see immediately attracts. Yet the sample explorations of this study may suggest that there is gold to be found. They may indicate that there are genuine resonances of the Spirit between separated Christians and between their traditions of faith. John Henry Newman's insight was a true one. Heart speaks to heart. *Laus Deo.*

NOTES

INTRODUCTION

1 J. Neville Ward, *Five for Sorrow, Ten for Joy: A Consideration of the Rosary*, Epworth 1979, p. xiii.
2 William H. Shannon, Introduction to Thomas Merton, *The Hidden Ground of Love: Letters of Religious Experience and Social Concerns*, Collins 1990, p. x.
3 *Unity Begins at Home:* A report from the first British Conference on Faith and Order, Nottingham 1964, 1964, p. 29
4 *Hymns and Psalms: A Methodist and Ecumenical Hymn Book*, Methodist Publishing House, 1983.

1: THE HEART IN PILGRIMAGE

1 *The Book of Common Worship*, Church of South India 1963, pp. 131–8.
2 Maldwyn L. Edwards, *Adam Clarke*, Wesley Historical Society Lecture No. 8, 1942, p. 40.
3 *Hymns and Psalms*, No. 540, verse 1.

2: THE MERSEY MIRACLE

1 For a detailed account of the growth of ecumenical partnership on Merseyside, see D. Worlock and D. Sheppard, *Better Together: Christian Partnership in a Hurt City*, Penguin 1989.

3: EDWARD KING AND UNITY IN CHRIST

1 B. W. Randolph, ed., *Spiritual Letters of Edward King*, 1910, p. 183.
2 Lord Elton, *Edward King and Our Times*, 1958, pp. 46–7.
3 F.E. Brightman, article on 'Edward King', in S. L. Ollard and G. Crosse, eds., *A Dictionary of English Church History*, 1912, p. 308.
4 Eric Graham, ed., *Pastoral Lectures of Bishop Edward King*, 1932, pp. ix, xiv.
5 ibid., p. 32.
6 G. W. E. Russell, *Edward King, Sixtieth Bishop of Lincoln*, 1912, p. 86.
7 *Spiritual Letters of Edward King*, p. 108.
8 *Pastoral Lectures of Bishop Edward King*, p. 12.

4: A TALE OF TWO BISHOPS

1 H. Scott Holland, *A Bundle of Memories*, 1915, p. 49.
2 For Sailer, see G. Schwaiger, *Johann Michael Sailer: Der bayerische Kirchenvater*, München/Zurich 1982.
3 A. Pütz, 'Bischof Edward King, ein anglikanischer Sailer-freund', in *Kurtrierisches Jahrbuch*, 1968, p. 294.
4 S. L. Ollard, ed., *A Forty Years' Friendship: Letters from the late Henry Scott Holland to Mrs. Drew*, 1919, p. 37.
5 J. M. Sailer, *Vorlesungen aus der Pastoraltheologie*, 3 Bde., Bd. 3, Preface.
6 J.M. Sailer, *Werke*, 42 Bde., 1830–1855, xx.301–302.
7 H. Küng, *The Church* (ET of *Die Kirche*, 1967), SCM 1968, p. 11. Küng writes: 'There is a world of difference between the ecclesiology of the Enlightenment which, basing itself on natural law, saw the Church from a juridical viewpoint as a *societas* having specific rights and obligations, and the later ecclesiology of Johann Michael Sailer which, under the influence of revivalist movements, mysticism and romanticism, concentrated above all on the religious and also the ethical side of the Church: the Church as the living mediatrix of a living spirituality.'
8 B. W. Randolph and J. W. Townroe, *The Mind and Work of Bishop King*, 1918, pp. 79–80.
9 B. W. Randolph, ed., Edward King, *Sermons and Addresses*, 1911, pp. 116–17.

10 E. F. Russell, ed., Edward King, *Counsels to Nurses*, 1911, Preface, pp. viii-ix.
11 ibid., pp. 49–50.
12 ibid., pp. 54–5.
13 ibid., p. 87.
14 Sailer, *Werke*, xviii.5–9.
15 E. Graham, ed., *Pastoral Lectures of Bishop Edward King*, p. 58.
16 Sailer, *Werke*, xviii. 22–3.
17 G.W.E. Russell, *Edward King*, pp. 125–6.
18 Sailer, *Werke*, xviii. 58–63.

5: THE HEART STRANGELY WARMED: A METHODIST RESPONSE TO ORTHODOXY

1 *The Works of John Wesley*, Vol. 18: W. R. Ward and R. P. Heitzenrater, eds. *Journal and Diaries* i (1735–38), 1988, pp. 249–50.
2 Julien Green, *Le Revenant: Journal* iii, *1946–52*, Paris 1958. (translation mine).
3 Constance Babington Smith, *Iulia de Beausobre: A Russian Christian in the West*, 1983, pp. 133–4.
4 A. M. Allchin, 'Our Life in Christ: in John Wesley and the Eastern Fathers', in A. M. Allchin, ed., *We Belong to One Another: Methodist, Anglican and Orthodox Essays*, 1965, p. 76.
5 *The Works of John Wesley*, Vol.7: F. Hildebrandt and O. A. Beckerlegge, eds., *A Collection of Hymns for the use of the People called Methodists*, 1983, pp. 436–7.
6 ibid., pp. 502–3.
7 ibid., pp. 592–3.
8 J. Telford, ed., *The Letters of the Rev. John Wesley A.M..*, 8 vols., 1931, viii. 238. (Letter of 15th September 1790).
9 See 2 Corinthians 6: 14–18.
10 John and Charles Wesley, *Hymns and Sacred Poems*, (1739), p. viii.
11 Symeon Lash: reference untraced.
12 G. Osborn, ed., *The Poetical Works of John and Charles Wesley*, 13 vols., London 1868–72, i.xxii.
13 John Wesley, *A Plain Account of Christian Perfection*, 1952 edn., p. 90.
14 *Works of John Wesley*, Vol. 7: *A Collection of Hymns*, p. 522.
15 John Wesley, *Explanatory Notes upon the New Testament* (1754), 1950 edn., p. 890.
16 *Hymns and Psalms* No. 109, verse 4.

17 ibid., No. 300, verse 2.
18 *Works of John Wesley*, Vol. 7: *A Collection of Hymns*, p. 693.
19 ibid., p. 694.
20 Cyril Davey, *The Glory Man: A new biography of Billy Bray*, Hodder 1974, pp. 65–6.
21 *Works of John Wesley*, Vol. 7: *A Collection of Hymns*, p. 328.
22 Cyril Davey, *The Glory Man*, p. 67.
23 Iulia de Beausobre, *Flame in the Snow*, 1979 edn., pp. 134–5.
24 ibid., p. 162.

6: METHODISM AND CATHOLICISM

1 Methodist Sacramental Fellowship, Pamphlet No. 7, *In Defence of the Methodist Sacramental Fellowship at the Conference of the Methodist Church at Hull, 1938*, n.d. Preface.
2 ibid., pp. 4–5.
3 ibid., p. 6. For John Scott Lidgett (1854–1953) see *The Dictionary of National Biography, 1951–1960*, pp. 633–5. The article on Lidgett is by Dr Harold Roberts, another distinguished Methodist ecumenist in the High Wesleyan tradition. Lidgett founded the Bermondsey Settlement (1891), became an Alderman of London County Council, and was Vice-Chancellor of London University 1930–32. He worked tirelessly for unity between the Free Churches and the Church of England. In both theology and social thought he was strongly influenced by F. D. Maurice.
4 J. E. Rattenbury, *In Defence of the Methodist Sacramental Fellowship*, p. 8.
5 Wesley Reprints, No. 1., *A Selection of Hymns on the Lord's Supper by John and Charles Wesley*, 1936, reprinted 1951.
6 See, for example, Timothy Dudley-Smith, *A Flame of Love: A Personal Choice of Charles Wesley's Verse*, Triangle 1987, pp. 88–90; and *A Rapture of Praise: hymns of John and Charles Wesley*, selected, arranged and introduced by H. A. Hodges and A. M. Allchin, 1966.
7 *Methodist Hymn Book*, 1933, No. 771, verse 3.
8 ibid., No. 723, verse 2.
9 *Hymns and Psalms*, No. 622, verse 2.
10 ibid., No. 621, verse 1.
11 ibid., No. 602, verse 1.
12 ibid., No. 298, verse 3.

13 See Alfred Cochrane's article, *Dictionary of National Biography, 1931–40*, p. 550.
14 A. E. Whitham, *The Catholic Christ*, 1940, p. 167.
15 ibid., pp. 174, 186.
16 T. S. Gregory, *According to your Faith*, 1966, p. 75. The blurb of the book, published by the (Methodist) Epworth Press, notes that: 'T. S. Gregory comes of a long line of Methodist ministers and was himself a Methodist minister for fourteen years. He then became a Roman Catholic without, as he says, ceasing to be a Methodist. He is still a student of the Wesleys and thinks that their great mission was to turn the life of ordinary people into a life of prayer.'
17 ibid., p. 76.

7: GRASPING THE NETTLE: THE ECUMENICAL SOCIETY OF THE BLESSED VIRGIN MARY

1 J. Neville Ward, *Five for Sorrow, Ten for Joy*, Preface, p. ix.
2 Walter M. Abbott and J. Gallagher, eds., *The Documents of Vatican II*, 1966, pp. 86, 88.
3 ibid., p. 90.
4 ibid., p. 92.
5 ibid., p. 95.
6 ibid., pp. 95–6.
7 *Hymns and Psalms*, No 87.
8 ibid., No. 126.

8: THE COMMON LIFE IN CHRIST

1 Works of John Wesley; Vol 7: *A Collection of Hymns*, p. 704.
2 See David Knowles, *The Religious Orders in England*, 3 vols., 1961–62, Vol. III *The Tudor Age*, pp. 231–3.
3 A. C. Outler, ed., *John Wesley*, in *A Library of Protestant Thought*, 1964, p. 8.
4 J. Telford, ed., *The Letters of the Rev. John Wesley, A.M.*, 8 vols., 1931, VI. 127–8.
5 ibid., VI. 6.
6 Outler, ed., *John Wesley*, p. 145.
7 *Works of John Wesley*, Vol. 7: *A Collection of Hymns*, p. 136.
8 ibid., p. 512.

9 J. E. Rattenbury, *The Evangelical Doctrines of Charles Wesley's Hymns*, 1941, p. 180.
10 *Works of John Wesley*, Vol. 7: *A Collection of Hymns*, pp. 707–8.
11 For a description of the Ashram Community, see John J. Vincent, *Radical Jesus*, 1986, pp. 105–7.
12 *Vision*, (Journal of the National Retreat Association), 1993, p. 5.

9: ONE IN THE SPIRIT: THE CHARISMATIC MOVEMENT AND THE CHURCHES

1 A. Marcus Ward to Marjorie Milne, 17th February 1966. Family Papers in Methodist Archives, John Rylands Library, Manchester. For Marcus Ward, see J. A. Newton, *A Man for All Churches: Marcus Ward*, 1984.
2 L. Newbigin, *The Household of God*, 1953, p. 89.
3 ibid., p. 87.
4 Kristina Cooper, 'How I Pray', *The Tablet*, 10th–17th April 1993, pp. 467–8.
5 L. J. Suenens, 'Spirit of Renewal', *The Tablet*, 19th September 1992, p. 1157.
6 ibid., p. 1157.
7 *Hymns and Psalms*, Preface, p. ix.
8 *Hymns and Psalms*, No. 326.
9 Walter J. Hollenweger, *The Pentecostals* (ET of German *Enthusiastiches Christentum: die Pfingstbewegung in Geschichte und Gegenwart*, 1969), Preface, p. xviii.
10 ibid., p. 7.
11 *The Tablet*, 24th April, 1993, p. 526.
12 John Wesley, *A Plain Account of Christian Perfection*, p. 90.